*You*

can minister

# SPIRITUAL GIFTS

**THOMAS W. ROYCROFT**
**Kenneth L. Fabbi, General Editor**

This is the original cover from the First Publication

**Publisher:**
**Kenneth L Fabbi**
**Lethbridge, Alberta, Canada**
**FiveFoldCycle@gmail.com**

**Copyright © 2019 Kenneth L. Fabbi**

First Published by Grape Press Publishing, Box 98, Throckmorton, Texas, 76083.

Second Publication Paper Chase (The Printing Factory) Inc., 3004 – 9 Avenue North, Lethbridge, Alberta.

Third Publication by Paper Boy Inc., 1502 – 2 Avenue South, Lethbridge, Alberta.
All rights reserved.

Unless otherwise indicated, all biblical quotations are taken from the New International Version (NIV) bible translation. The majority of Thomas W. Roycroft's original bible references were in King James Version (KJV) or Authorized Version of the King James (AV). Many references have been left in the original.

The Holy Bible, New International Version®, NIV® Copyright © 1973, 1978, 1984, 2011 by Biblica, Inc.® Used by permission. All rights reserved worldwide.

21st Century King James Version®, Copyright © 1994. Used by permission of Deuel Enterprises, Inc., Gary, SD 57237. All rights reserved.

Weymouth New Testament (WNT), otherwise known as *The New Testament in Modern Speech 1903 & 1909.*

Young's Literal Translation (YLT) 1862.

Any Internet Address (websites, email, etc.) printed in this book are offered as a resource. They are not intended in any way to be or imply an endorsement by Kenneth L Fabbi Publishing.

No part of this publication may be reproduced in any form, or by any means, electronic, including photocopying, recording, or any information browsing, storage, or retrieval system, without permission in writing from the General Editor. Kenneth would welcome your communication at FiveFoldCycle@gmail.com.

**ISBN:**
**Paperback ISBN: 978-0-9952039-3-8**
**eBook ISBN:  978-0-9952039-4-5**

**Subjects:    Christianity - - Holy Spirit -**
**Growth - - Spiritual Gifts**

**I. Title    II. Roycroft, Thomas W.**
**III. Fabbi, Kenneth L.**

# TABLE OF CONTENTS

**GENERAL EDITOR'S NOTES** .................. 9

**ACKNOWLEDGEMENTS:** ..................... 9

**INTRODUCTION TO THE SPIRITUAL GIFTS** ...... 11

**TONGUES IS EVIDENCE OF THE BAPTISM IN THE SPIRIT** ........................................ 15

**REFLECT ON THE BAPTISM IN THE SPIRIT** ........ 19

**UNDERSTANDING THE SPIRITUAL GIFTS** ......... 21

**WHEN OPERATING SPIRITUAL GIFTS** ............ 25

**HOW MANY GIFTS MAY A BELIEVER HAVE?** ...... 27

**THE GIFTS FALL INTO THREE GROUPS OF THREE** 30

**THE OPERATION OF SPIRITUAL GIFTS** ............ 31


**CHAPTER ONE – THE GIFT OF THE WORD OF WISDOM** ................................. 34


**CHAPTER TWO – THE GIFT OF THE WORD OF KNOWLEDGE** ............................ 37

THE WORD OF KNOWLEDGE COMES IN VARIOUS WAYS ................................. 38

HOW DO I GET IT TO WORK? .................. 41

EXCEPTIONS .................................. 43

IMPORTANT – TO MAINTAIN THE OPERATION OF THIS GIFT AND ALL THE GIFTS ............. 44

## CHAPTER THREE – THE GIFT OF DISCERNING OF SPIRITS .................... 45
BY THIS GIFT WE CAN DISCERN .................. 48
SATAN AND HIS SPIRITS CAN BE DIVIDED INTO THREE GROUPS ................................. 49

## CHAPTER FOUR – THE GIFT OF TONGUES .. 52
WHEN I EXERCISE THE GIFT OF TONGUES ....... 55

## CHAPTER FIVE – THE GIFT OF INTERPRETATION OF TONGUES ...................... 60

## CHAPTER SIX – THE GIFT OF PROPHECY ... 62
THOSE WHO BENEFIT FROM PROPHECY ......... 66
PROPORTION OF FAITH ........................ 67
SOME OF THE THINGS THAT PROPHECY IS NOT .. 68

## CHAPTER SEVEN – THE GIFT OF FAITH .... 70
THREE KINDS OF FAITH ........................ 70
FAITH OF GOD EXAMINED ...................... 72
FAITH COMETH BY HEARING THE WORD OF GOD 74

## CHAPTER EIGHT – GIFTS OF HEALING ..... 75
STAGES OF DEMONIC INFLUENCE ............... 76
HEALING IN THE ATONEMENT .................. 77
METHODS OF DIVINE HEALING .................. 79
STORY OF MR. X .............................. 82

HEALING THROUGH REPENTANCE AND
FORGIVENESS .................................. 86

PRACTICAL STEPS TO FORGIVENESS ........... 88

HEALING BY THE WORD OF COMMAND ........ 88

ATTENTION READER .......................... 89

**CHAPTER NINE – THE GIFT OF MIRACLES 90**

FOUR STEPS TO A MIRACLE .................... 90
FOUR STEPS TO A MIRACLE EXPLAINED ........ 92
THE TWO FOLD POWER OF THE WORD OF GOD . 96
HOW DO YOU KEEP FROM DOUBTING IN YOUR
HEART? .......................................... 99
EXPECT A MIRACLE .......................... 103

**CHAPTER TEN – THE MIRACLE OF
RAISING THE DEAD ...................... 107**

**CHAPTER ELEVEN – CASTING OUT
DEVILS ..................................... 111**

EDITOR'S NOTE: THE AUTHOR'S LIST OF
EXPECTATIONS OF BELIEVER. ................ 114
PROCEDURE WHEN CASTING OUT DEVILS. ..... 115
CONCLUSION ................................ 117

**NOTES ........................................ 119**

**APPENDIX ONE:**

**UNDERSTANDING THE GIFTS ........... 121**

**APPENDIX TWO:**
**PRAYER FOR THE BAPTISM IN THE SPIRIT 124**
THE PRAYER .................................. 125

**APPENDIX THREE:**
**BRIEF BIOGRAPHY OF THOMAS WILLIAM ROYCROFT ............................. 127**

# GENERAL EDITOR'S NOTES:

The original document by Thomas 'Tom' Roycroft, offers a well planned and useful explanation of the Spiritual Gifts and how each individual can minister the Spiritual Gifts. In his writing he used capital letters to emphasis important points. I have left them as is. As well he made many scripture references, statements and conclusions in the work: some of these I have expanded to assist the reader.

My thanks go out to the Roycroft Family for the opportunity to get this material out where it can be found by the wider population. It is my hope that it will be a blessing to you and to those with whom you share it.

*God Bless you.* Kenneth Fabbi

# ACKNOWLEDGEMENTS:

As I edited this book, I invited a number of people to review different portions and comment. We tried to stay faithful to Tom's original work, but allow for what we have learned and experienced in our work with the Holy Spirit.

I would like to especially thank Gerben and Gardien Terpstra for their energy and time, especially in trying to understand Tongues as evidence of The Baptism In

The Spirit. It is always a gift to have Gerben and Gardien's support and prayer.

Thank you Peter Kallen for reviewing the text and correcting my oversights. I appreciate you!

As well I would like to thank June Tymensen and Sherry Rohovie, who painstakingly went through the material and offered suggestions, punctuation and order. They captured Tom's idea that this material was a 'course' and in that understanding, we added material to guide the reader.

# INTRODUCTION TO THE SPIRITUAL GIFTS

Tom explained that this course is undoubtedly the best of its kind up to the present. Other courses on Spiritual Gifts have dealt with WHAT the Bible characters did. THIS COURSE GIVES A CLEAR UNDERSTANDING OF HOW THEY DID IT, AND HOW YOU CAN ENTER INTO A POWERFUL AND EFFECTIVE GIFT MINISTRY.

Paul in Corinthians gives an overview of the Spiritual Gifts, telling the Corinthians that he does not want them to be uninformed.

> **[1] Now about the gifts of the Spirit, brothers and sisters, I do not want you to be uninformed. [2] You know that when you were pagans, somehow or other you were influenced and led astray to mute idols. [3] Therefore I want you to know that no one who is speaking by the Spirit of God says, "Jesus be cursed," and no one can say, "Jesus is Lord," except by the Holy Spirit.**
>
> **[4] There are different kinds of gifts, but the same Spirit distributes them. [5] There are different kinds of service, but the same Lord. [6] There are different kinds of working, but in all of them and in everyone it is the same God at work. [7] Now to each one the manifestation of the Spirit is given for the common good. [8] To one there is given**

**through the Spirit a message of wisdom, to another a message of knowledge by means of the same Spirit, [9] to another faith by the same Spirit, to another gifts of healing by that one Spirit, [10] to another miraculous powers, to another prophecy, to another distinguishing between spirits, to another speaking in different kinds of tongues, and to still another the interpretation of tongues. [11] All these are the work of one and the same Spirit, and he distributes them to each one, just as he determines.**
1 Corinthians 12: 1-11

Why are spiritual gifts necessary? Because gifts strengthen and build up believers spiritually, and because gifts convince unbelievers by DEMONSTRATING THE SUPERNATURAL.

According to Paul, the Gospel is not FULLY proclaimed unless it is preached with signs, miracles and healings. Paul explains this in Romans:

**[18] I will not venture to speak of anything except what Christ has accomplished through me in leading the Gentiles to obey God by what I have said and done— [19] by the power of signs and wonders, through the power of the Spirit of God. So from Jerusalem all the way around to Illyricum, I have fully proclaimed the gospel of Christ. [20] It has always been my ambition to preach the gospel where Christ was not known, so that I would not be building on someone else's foundation.**
Romans 15:18 - 20

Paul's preaching was in demonstration of the Spirit and power of God (1 Corinthians 2: 4). This power through the Spirit was demonstrated in Acts. Read carefully Acts 8: 6.

> **⁶ When the crowds heard Philip and SAW THE SIGNS HE PREFORMED, they all PAID CLOSE ATTENTION to what he said.**
> Acts 8: 6

Not only did the people hear the word, they also saw the miracles, and as a result, they believed.

According to Jesus, signs are to accompany the preaching of the Gospel.

> **¹⁷ And these signs will accompany those who believe: In my name they will drive out demons; they will speak in new tongues; ¹⁸ they will pick up snakes with their hands; and when they drink deadly poison, it will not hurt them at all; they will place their hands on sick people, and they will get well.**
> Mark 16: 17-18

An unbelieving world has a right to demand proof. The signs are OUR CREDENTIALS – proof that the Word preached is the truth, proof that the Lord is risen and is Himself confirming the Word by the signs which accompany the preaching. Some good, sincere people will cry out, "Don't ask for proof. Just believe!" But the Lord Jesus Christ when challenged, pointed to His signs, miracles and healings – His divine credentials – as a BASIS FOR FAITH.

> **² When John, who was in prison, heard about the deeds of the Messiah, he sent his disciples ³ to ask him, "Are you the one who is to come, or should we expect someone else?" ⁴ Jesus replied, "Go back and report to John what you hear and see: ⁵ The blind receive sight, the lame walk, those who have leprosy are cleansed, the deaf hear, the dead are raised, and the good news is proclaimed to the poor."**
> Matthew 11: 2-5

Jesus did not do miracles 'on demand' to prove who He was. He pointed to His past works to speak for Him.

> **²⁵ Jesus answered, "I did tell you, but you do not believe. The works I do in my Father's name testify about me,"**
> John 10: 25

This, the supernatural in demonstration, was the power of the early church (Hebrews 2:4); and according to Mark 16:15-18 these supernatural signs, miracles and healings are to continue as long as the Gospel is preached and as long as men become believers.

Signs do make a difference today. A few years ago, one of the world's best known evangelists was challenged in Africa to demonstrate the power of God. He chose to decline; and that African campaign was a failure. Thomas Osborn[1], (Tommy Lee Osborn 1923-2013), when confronted with a similar situation in the midst of fanatical African Moslems, said, "Send up a man to the platform that God may heal him, and you will know that this preaching is of God." A deaf priest stepped up and was healed immediately. As a result of this miracle a great multitude were swept into the kingdom of God just as in the days of the early church.

Mighty works and miracles DO NOT occur, however, unless believers are BAPTIZED IN THE HOLY GHOST. And here may we point out that being filled with the Holy Spirit is not to be lightly regarded as a matter of individual choice. The Bible enjoins it upon ALL (Ephesians 5:18) and Jesus commanded his disciples NOT to preach the Gospel until they were filled with the Spirit. (Luke 24:49; Acts 1:4-8).

> **[48] You are witnesses of these things. [49] I am going to send you what my Father has promised; but stay in the city until you have been clothed with power from on high."**
> Luke 24:48-49

This is the last commandment given by Jesus before He ascended up into Heaven: that we are to be clothed with the power from on high – His Holy Spirit.

## TONGUES IS EVIDENCE OF THE BAPTISM IN THE SPIRIT

The ONLY Holy Ghost baptism is the baptism accompanied by the supernatural experience of SPEAKING IN OTHER TONGUES. This is the Bible standard and it changes not.

Tom Roycroft was quite clear in his writing and preaching, that Tongues was the only clear evidence of the Baptism in the Spirit. This conclusion lead him and others of his time to conclude 'no Gift of Tongues – no Baptism in the Spirit'. This Editor has found this to be *inaccurate*.

Tom explained his argument as follows: The disciples before the day of Pentecost had experienced manifestations of faith or miracles or supernatural revelation. Nevertheless, they had not been filled with the Holy Ghost. How do we know? Because Jesus, after He rose from the dead, told them to WAIT until they received the baptism of the Holy Spirit. Therefore, signs, healings, preaching, casting out devils and Divine revelations cannot be regarded as evidence of the baptism of the Spirit.

Listen to the Word;

> **[4] And they were all filled with the Holy Ghost, and began to SPEAK WITH OTHER TONGUES, as the Spirit gave them utterance.**
> Acts 2:4 KJV

So, there is but one evidence - tongues. Peter referred to the outpouring of the Spirit as:

> **"THIS which ye now SEE and HEAR".**
> Acts 2:33 KJV

What did they see? People being filled with the Spirit. What did they hear? Tongues. So, speaking in other tongues was the evidence. We read that in the house of Cornelius, the Gentile, it was the speaking in other tongues which convinced Peter and his Jewish brethren.

> **[45] The circumcised believers who had come with Peter were astonished that the gift of the Holy Spirit had been poured out even on Gentiles. [46] For they heard them speaking in tongues and praising God. Then Peter said, [47] "Surely no one can stand in the way of their being baptized with**

water. They have received the Holy Spirit just as we have."
Acts 10:45-47

And later when Peter returned home, it was this same supernatural phenomenon of speaking in other languages which silenced the objections of the skeptical saints in Jerusalem and convinced them that the Spirit had indeed fallen upon the Gentiles.

Peter said:

> **15 "As I began to speak, THE HOLY SPIRIT CAME ON THEM AS HE HAD COME ON US at the beginning. 16 Then I remembered what the Lord had said: 'John baptized with water, but you will be baptized with the Holy Spirit.' 17 So if God gave them THE SAME GIFT he gave us who believed in the Lord Jesus Christ, who was I to think that I could stand in God's way?" 18 When they heard this, they had no further objections and praised God, saying, "So then, even to Gentiles God has granted repentance that leads to life."**
> Acts 11:15-18

Twenty-one years later at Ephesus, the evidence of the baptism of the Holy Spirit was still the same.

> **6 When Paul placed his hands on them, the HOLY SPIRIT came on them, AND they spoke in tongues and prophesied.**
> Acts 19:6

Nor did tongues cease with the Apostles. Bishop Irenaeus mentions it in the second century, and Saint Augustine wrote as follows in the fourth century, "We still do what the Apostles did when they laid hands upon believers and called down the Holy Ghost upon them. IT IS EXPECTED that converts shall speak in new tongues."

Tom Roycroft concludes that Tongues is clear evidence that someone has received the Holy Spirit, but he went on to make a more definitive statement. To sum up: No tongues, no Holy Ghost baptism. No spiritual gifts, no tools to do the job. No tools to do the job, a job poorly done or not done at all. Experience has shown this conclusion to be *inaccurate*.

Roycroft concluded that one has not received the Holy Spirit, if that person does not have the evidence of Tongues. This Editor has found this not to be true in both my personal experience and my life experiences. It is possible to receive the Baptism in the Holy Spirit and yet Tongues is not activated or blocked.

Roycroft softens this conclusion in this next paragraph.

Because a believer has a good measure of God's Spirit some of the nine spiritual gifts may be present in a measure and may even operate to a limited extent, but a believer cannot - I repeat CANNOT - speak in other tongues unless he has been baptized in the Holy Ghost. THEN with the FULNESS of the Spirit ALL of the nine spiritual gifts can function in their fullness.

**Editor's Conclusions from this discussion:**
It is clear that the conclusive evidence of receiving the Baptism in the Spirit is the Gift of Tongues, but this

does not preclude the possibility that one might receive other Gifts and be active in other Gifts, such as Knowledge, Wisdom and Discernment and not yet have opened to the Gift of Tongues. This was true in the life of this Editor. I, Kenneth, received the Baptism in the Spirit in 1984, with active Gifts of Knowledge, Wisdom, Prophesy and Discernment, yet did not activate the Gift of Tongues until the Summer of 1986, two years later.

## REFLECT ON THE BAPTISM IN THE SPIRIT:

Tongues is a sign – it gives evidence of the Baptism in the Spirit. Like all the Gifts, openness to the Gift is necessary for the gift to activate and it is possible to activate one gift yet be closed off to another. We have found that the manifestation of the gifts and the order of their presentation are unique to the individual. Tongue is often the gateway in moving in the other gifts. It facilitates their operation.

One should also realize that the Spiritual Gifts come with the Gift of the Holy Spirit. When Jesus told his followers to wait for the Father's Gift, Jesus was talking about the Baptism in the Holy Spirit.

> **[4] On one occasion, while he was eating with them, he gave them this command: "Do not leave Jerusalem, but wait for the gift my Father promised, which you have heard me speak about. [5] For John baptized with water, but in a few days you will be baptized with the Holy Spirit."**
> Acts 1:4-5

Jesus spoke about this Gift a number of times. Each time the Gift He was speaking about was not broken into the Gifts of the Spirit, but one Gift and one Gift only; that being the Gift of the Holy Spirit.

> **[26] But the Advocate, the Holy Spirit, whom the Father will send in my name, will teach you all things and will remind you of everything I have said to you.**
> John 14: 26

> **[13] But when he, the Spirit of truth, comes, he will guide you into all the truth. He will not speak on his own; he will speak only what he hears, and he will tell you what is yet to come.**
> John 16: 13

> **[8] But you will receive power when the Holy Spirit comes on you; and you will be my witnesses in Jerusalem, and in all Judea and Samaria, and to the ends of the earth.**
> Acts 1: 8

We tend to individualize gifts of the Spirit, but the reality is that the Gift from the Father is the gift of the Holy Spirit, in whom all the gifts reside.

Baptism in the Holy Spirit is one Gift with many manifestations. We are to be immersed in the Holy Spirit: filled with the Holy Spirit. God is Spirit and therefore we are immersed in God: baptized into – immersed into Him. As one friend of mine says, we are to 'let go and let God".

God's Spirit is to dwell within us: within our Temple. As scriptures says our body is the Temple of the Holy Spirit.

> **¹⁹ Do you not know that your bodies are temples of the Holy Spirit, who is in you, whom you have received from God? You are not your own;**
>
> 1 Corinthians 6: 19

Immersed in the Spirit, Baptized in the Spirit, refers to a willful decision to invite God's Spirit to dwell within us and to rule our lives – to rule our body, soul and spirit.

> **¹³ If you then, though you are evil, know how to give good gifts to your children, how much more will your Father in heaven give the Holy Spirit to those who ask him!"**
> Luke 11:13

Another factor in the scale of having the Spirit or no Spirit, is the Rule of Love or Role of Love. Spiritual Gifts are dependent on Love (1 Corinthians 13: 1-13). Love is the most important measuring stick. To be in the Spirit we must be proved by Love (John 16: 7-11). If you are not proved by Love then you are not acting in the Spirit.

# UNDERSTANDING THE SPIRITUAL GIFTS

According to 1 Corinthians 12:7 each gift is a MANIFESTATION or showing forth of the Holy Spirit who dwells in the believer. The Holy Spirit dwells within you (John 14:17) having come in to abide or remain (1 John 2:27 & John 14:16). These gifts are WITHIN YOU

(See 2 Timothy 1:6) and will not be taken away from you (Romans 11:29).

Read carefully 1 Peter 4:10-11.

> **¹⁰ Each of you should use whatever gift you have received to serve others, as faithful stewards of God's grace in its various forms. ¹¹ If anyone speaks, they should do so as one who speaks the very words of God. If anyone serves, they should do so with the strength God provides, so that in all things God may be praised through Jesus Christ. To him be the glory and the power for ever and ever. Amen.**
> 1 Peter 4:10-11

Here Peter speaks of ministering spiritual gifts to the needs of men. In the Greek, the word gift is charisma (kar-is-ma). Not only does it mean a gift, but it also conveys the meaning of 'special power or endowment', 'rights granted to a person', 'capacity or qualification for any action'.

This manifestation of God's 'grace' in the believer is, 'manifold', dividing in its operation into nine spiritual gifts. These gifts we "minister as of the ABILITY WHICH GOD GIVETH" (1 Peter 4:11 KJV). In other words, we are ministering God-given abilities. Therefore, it is correct to say that:

## A GIFT IS A GOD GIVEN ABILITY

The word rendered 'ability' in this passage has in the original Greek the meaning of 'strength'. In this case, however, the word 'ability' expressed the true meaning because a God-given strength is a Divinely-imparted ABILITY. It enables you to do the job!

Why do we emphasize this point? Because you must realize that these spiritual gifts are not something away off somewhere, but God-given abilities which you HAVE and which are WITHIN YOU. Peter said,

> **"WHAT I HAVE, this I give thee".**
> Acts 3:6 KJV

Just as you have and use natural abilities, so you move in by faith and use your God-given spiritual abilities when there is a need of them.

Gifts are good, perfect, and come down from the unchanging One (James 1:17, Matthew 7:11). They are without repentance or recall - irrevocable.

> **29 for God's gifts and his call are irrevocable.**
> Romans 11:29

They are as precious stones to the user (Proverbs 17:8).

> **8 A gift is as a precious stone in the eyes of him that hath it: whithersoever it turneth, it prospereth.**
> Proverbs 17:8 KJV

A man's gift makes room and opens the way for him (Proverbs 18:16).

> **16 A gift opens the way and ushers the giver into the presence of the great.**
> Proverbs 18:16

St Paul told us that:

- we are not to be ignorant of spiritual gifts (1 Corinthians 12:1).

  **12 Now about the gifts of the Spirit, brothers and sisters, I do not want you to be uninformed.**
  1 Corinthians 12:1

- the Gifts are not to be neglected (1 Timothy 4:14).

  **14 Do not neglect your gift, which was given you through prophecy when the body of elders laid their hands on you.**
  1 Timothy 4:14

- they are to be desired (1 Corinthians 12:31)

  **31 Now eagerly desire the greater gifts.**
  1 Corinthians 12:31

- the Gifts are to be stirred up (2 Timothy 1:6)

  **6 For this reason I remind you to fan into flames the gift of God, which is in you through the laying on of hands.**
  2 Timothy 1:6

- they are to be ministered (1 Peter 4:10).

  **10 Each of you should use whatever gift you have received to serve others, as faithful stewards of God's grace in its various forms.**
  1 Peter 4:10

Spiritual gifts establish believers (Romans 1:11). They are a source of profit to all (1 Corinthians 12:7). They impart to others faith, blessing, healing and deliverance

(Acts 2:4-21 - Pentecost). They make obedient by word and deed (Romans 15:18). They are our credentials and are for confirmation of the Word. (Mark 16:17-20). They glorify God (1 Peter 4:11).

Gifts are by the GRACE of God which is given to YOU. (1 Corinthians 1:4, 5; 1 Peter 4:10).

The gifts are DIFFERENT one from another (1 Corinthians 12:4) though they work in combinations and supplement one another as in the case of the Word of Knowledge and the Word of Wisdom.

Gifts in varying combinations are operative in "DIFFERENT ADMINISTRATIONS" (1 Corinthians 12:5 AV), or official ministries in the church (1 Corinthians 12:5).

Gifts are DIFFERENT in OPERATION (working) in the case of each individual. (1 Corinthians 12:6) Therefore do not expect your gifts to operate in the same manner as the gifts of another; and don't get into a rut and expect your gifts to always operate exactly as they did previously. Let the Spirit have complete liberty to be different in His working; and expect new things from time to time.

## WHEN OPERATING SPIRITUAL GIFTS:

1. "OBEY the moving of the Spirit
2. which operates ACCORDING TO THE WORD
3. on the BASIS of LOVE".

Read this sentence again and again throughout the course. Tom says it was given by revelation to a friend of mine.

Meditate upon it; pray about it; and then read it again. Better still; continue to use this three point message to CHECK on your Christian walk and your gift ministry from time to time.

If you fail to keep in mind this rule you may become like others – and their name is legion – who somehow or other have 'gone off the beam', bringing reproach upon spiritual gifts and the Name of Christ. If, on the other hand, you consistently follow this rule, you can have a powerful ministry, honored of God, feared by the Devil, sought after and respected by saint and sinner.

We have just stated that "THE GIFT IS THE GOD GIVEN ABILITY TO PERFORM THE ACT".

This is gloriously true; but may I sound a warning here? The gift is not a God given ability to perform the act APART FROM the will of God, but a God given ability to act ACCORDING TO HIS WILL. Some have made spiritual shipwreck of themselves and others by regarding spiritual gifts as a kind of gimmick to be freely used in self-will and self-interest.

Whenever possible aim to know God's will (obtain His blueprint for the job) before you minister spiritual gifts. If, however, there is a need apparent or expressed, and to meet that need would seem to be according to the written Word and to God's glory – and God hasn't shown you NOT to minister – then go ahead not doubting. You are not ministering gifts in self-will but committing all things to God that He may guide the outcome – and He will.

The Bible says.

> **"Desire spiritual gifts."**
> (1 Corinthians 14:1)
>
> **"Covet the best gifts"**
> (1 Corinthians 12:31 KJV)

(Tom add this interesting phrase: "that is, the gifts which are the best for your ministry".)

# HOW MANY GIFTS MAY A BELIEVER HAVE?

This brings us to the question "How many gifts may a believer have?"

If each of the nine spiritual gifts is a manifestation of the indwelling Holy Spirit (1 Corinthians 12:7), then it follows that the nine gifts are resident in the Holy Spirit; and if the nine gifts are resident in the Holy Spirit, then all Spirit-filled believers potentially have the nine gifts. Sometimes certain gifts begin to operate naturally. When this is not the case, gifts maybe imparted, or liberty for their operation be imparted, by the laying on of hands (2 Timothy 1:6; Romans 1:11).

Some years ago I, Tom, ministered to a lady who had three spiritual gifts in operation and desired more. God gave me a vision of a house with nine windows. The light was streaming from three of the windows but the other six had shutters on them. All that was necessary was to GET THE SHUTTERS OFF!

Some will use 1 Corinthians 12:29, 30, in an effort to prove that believers cannot have all of the nine gifts. They glibly quote, "Do all speak with tongues? Do all interpret? Have all the gifts of healing?" But Paul is not speaking here of gifts but of the various MINISTRIES of members in the church (verses 27 and 28) – the ministry of an apostle, the ministry of a prophet, the ministry of a teacher, the ministry of one who in the church gives messages in tongues, the ministry of one who gives interpretation of such messages, the ministry of one who heals the sick. Each one has a different ministry therefore let each believer "covet earnestly the best gifts" for HIS particular ministry.

(I, Tom, may add that the above explanation also answers those who in ignorance would try to make 1 Corinthians 12: 28 & 30 say that the GIFT of tongues is not for all).

The exponents of the 'one gift per man' teaching will also quote 1 Corinthians 12:11 to prove their point. Let us read this passage again carefully. Note that it is not the GIFTS which are divided to each individual, here one gift and there another, but the SPIRIT that divides HIMSELF to each believer as on the day of Pentecost. (Acts 2:3) The Corinthians, newly converted and with a heathen background, were familiar with the workings of MANY spirits. Paul emphasizes here, as in verse 4, that the Holy Spirit is ONE spirit dividing and working in each believer according to His will.

Paul, himself, had the nine gifts, plus special miracles (Acts 19:11).

He had:

The gift of the Word of Wisdom (2 Peter 3:15)

The gift of the Word of Knowledge (Acts 13:11)

The gift of Discerning of Spirits (Acts 16:16-18; 14:9)

The gift of Tongues (1 Corinthians 14:18)

The gift of Interpretation (1 Corinthians 14:13)

The gift of Prophecy (1 Corinthians 14:6)

The gift of Faith to work signs and wonders (Romans 15, 18, 19)

The gift of Healings (Acts 14:8-10)

The gift of Miracles (Acts 20:9-12)

# THE GIFTS FALL INTO THREE GROUPS OF THREE

**REVELATION GIFTS**
(Gifts to KNOW) (The Ability to KNOW.)

> Word of Wisdom
> Word of Knowledge
> Discerning of Spirits

NOTE:
When the revelation is received, it must be ACTED UPON.


**UTTERANCE OR VOICE GIFTS**
(Gifts to SPEAK) (The Ability to SAY.)

> Tongues
> Interpretation
> Prophesy


**POWER GIFTS**
(Gifts to ACT)  (The Ability to DO.)

> Faith
> Healings
> Miracles

These last three are called POWER GIFTS because they operate by God's power (Romans 15:18-19). Remember, THE POWER IS IN US (Romans 9:17; Acts 1:8; Ephesians 3:20; Romans 8:11).

Refer to Appendix One, *Understanding The Gifts,* for an explanation of the nine gifts. This outline can be used to teach the gifts.

# THE OPERATION OF SPIRITUAL GIFTS

First realize this: You must be TRANSPARENTLY HONEST before God, SEEKING TO OBEY FROM THE HEART EVERY PART OF GOD'S WORD. Otherwise somewhere down the road there is a danger of two things: Your own mind and thoughts will intrude more and more into Revelation, Word of Knowledge and Prophesy; and worse still, "a strong (Satanic) delusion" (2 Thessalonians 2:11) may move in to contaminate and mislead. God's gifts are not something to be trifled with.

Jesus said of himself:

> **"The Prince of this world
> cometh and hath nothing in Me".**
> John 14:30 KJV

Apply this to yourself, Believer. No thing in me – no hatred, no jealousy, no roots of bitterness, no pride – nothing that the Devil can use to hinder my being FULLY YIELDED to and CONTROLLED by the Holy

Spirit, whose presence in me is manifested in spiritual gifts.

Now you stand in God's presence to do His work. You recall His revealed word to one of His servants:

### "I have given to you the ability to enter and to work and to war in the spirit realm at WILL."

(This prophetic word is confirmed by a number of scriptures including: Luke 10:19, Luke 9:1, 2 Corinthians 10: 3-5, & Ephesians 6:10-17)

You speak aloud or perhaps inaudibly in tongues because "tongues are a bridge into the spiritual realm".

You are shutting out everything you know in your natural mind, shutting out your own will and the will of others. You want only His will and His word being revealed within you. You are shut in with God so that down in the depths of your spirit where He dwells, you may inquire and hear and know. You are a vessel filled with Him; you are a channel for His gifts to operate through according to His working which worketh in you mightily – a CO-WORKER WITH GOD (1 Corinthians 3:9 KJV, Colossians 1: 29 KJV).

Perhaps you used to think that a gift was something which you must reach out for and receive from God each time that there was a need to be met. Now you know better. Instead of praying, "Father give me this gift I need this gift now", you will whisper in your heart, "Father, this gift, which you have put within is now going to operate for Your glory". Then, automatically, you will find yourself moving in faith and operating that supernatural God-given ability just as unconsciously as you would a natural ability.

Each and every gift operates by faith. By faith you know that that the gift is within you. By faith you ACT, thus releasing the gift so that the job may be done.

What if there comes a time when the gifts do not operate freely because you have been passing through a period of spiritual drought? Here is a case where YOU must take DRASTIC ACTION to lay hold on God. You must STIR UP the gifts by prayer, by reading the Word and by speaking in other tongues (2 Timothy 1:6).

> **⁶ Wherefore I put thee in remembrance that thou STIR UP THE GIFT OF GOD, which is in thee by the putting on of my hands.**
> 2 Timothy 1:6 KJV

In the NIV it is translated "fan into flames".

> **⁶ For this reason I remind you to fan into flame the gift of God, which is in you through the laying on of my hands.**
> 2 Timothy 1:6

The gifts are there. They are yours, God will not take them from you. STIR THEM UP.

# CHAPTER ONE
# THE GIFT OF THE
# WORD OF WISDOM
# 1 Corinthians 12:

The Word of Wisdom is just what the Bible declares it to be – a word or portion of Divine wisdom. It is 'wisdom given', a gift from God to man. (2 Peter 3:15)

Natural wisdom, according to the dictionary definition, is "the ability to apply possessed knowledge and experience."

THE GIFT OF THE WORD OF WISDOM IS THE GOD-GIVEN ABILITY TO RECEIVE SUPERNATURAL WISDOM FROM GOD AT A TIME WHEN WISDOM IS NEEDED.

It enables the possessor of the gift to wisely USE either natural knowledge or Divinely imparted knowledge.

It is the Lord who gives this wisdom (Proverbs 2:6) and it is not to be classed with natural human wisdom which originates in the mind. It is a manifestation of supernatural, Divine wisdom to man's spirit. The Bible says, "When wisdom is entered into thine HEART" (Proverbs 2:10 KJV; 1 Kings 10:24). When a believer is full of the Holy Ghost this gift frequently operates spontaneously as a spoken word, it is not only in the heart but in the TONGUE, and it comes without delay and without premeditation. (See Luke 21:14, 15)

In the realm of the Spirit and in the affairs of God's people there should be no place for human wisdom which too often is open to the direction of the Satanic powers of this world. James 3:15-17 KJV clearly outlines the Devil's counterfeit of God's gift. This wisdom is not from above. It is "earthly" (as opposed to heavenly) "sensual" (according to sense knowledge) and "devilish" (abounding in applied psychology, expediency, human conniving, selfish, materialistic reasoning and scheming – all of which have their roots in the pit). Example: the wisdom which Jesus' enemies used against Him.

Carnal Christians are often tempted to use this kind of wisdom in church affairs. Result: "envy, strife, confusion and EVERY evil work". (James 3:16 KJV)

To combat this, use God's wisdom. That is what Jesus did! Back it up with the AUTHORITY OF THE BELIEVER boldly exercised in faith and you will prevail.

Read 1 Corinthians, chapter two, slowly and carefully. The wisdom Paul is speaking of is the mind of Christ, and "we have the mind of Christ" because He dwells WITHIN and reveals His mind (His will, His thoughts) by a Word of Knowledge and by a Word of Wisdom. "In Him are hid ALL the treasures of wisdom and knowledge – and ye are COMPLETE IN HIM." COLOSSIANS 2: 3,9,10 KJV)

> **"THEREFORE if any man lack WISDOM let him ASK of God who giveth to all men liberally AND IT SHALL BE GIVEN HIM". "But let him ask in FAITH, nothing wavering."** James 1:5, 6 KJV

You receive the Word of Wisdom just as you receive the Word of Knowledge. (See below: The Word of Knowledge Comes In Various Ways ) These two gifts are closely related, working together in the Word of God. The Word of Knowledge may be regarded as the storeroom and the Word of Wisdom as the exit door for unloading.

This gift is put FIRST – ahead of all the other gifts. We need God's wisdom to witness acceptably, to correct the erring, to answer those who would twist our words, to bring forth This gift is put FIRST – ahead of all the other gifts. We need God's wisdom to witness acceptably, to correct the erring, to answer those who would twist our words, to bring forth revelations, and to 'get along' with our fellow man. In our relations with saint and sinner, Divine wisdom is what we need most – more than we need the Gift of Miracles.

# CHAPTER TWO
# THE GIFT OF THE WORD OF KNOWLEDGE
# 1 Corinthians 12: 8

The gift of the Word of Knowledge is not natural sense knowledge. It is not the learning, education, psychology or wisdom of this world. It is not fortune telling which is the Devil's counterfeit of God's gift. Nor is it a knowledge of God which comes by learning or by study or by many years of experience with the ways of God. Above all it is not 'the gift of knowledge', as many wrongly term it, for that would put at our disposal ALL of the knowledge of God. It is what the Bible calls it – "a word", a portion of God's knowledge. (1 Corinthians 13:9-10)

THE GIFT OF THE WORD OF KNOWLEDGE IS THE GOD-GIVEN ABILITY TO RECEIVE FROM GOD BY REVELATION FACTS AND INFORMATION WHICH IT IS HUMANLY IMPOSSIBLE TO KNOW.

This God-given ability to know the humanly unknowable when necessary is something which is absolutely essential to the believer both in his service to God and in matters requiring personal guidance. The Word of Knowledge takes over where natural knowledge fails.

Sometimes the operation of this gift is unexpected and entirely involuntary so far as we are concerned. There is some need of which we are not aware and by means of a Word of Knowledge God reveals His will, warns us of danger, prepares us for some emergency or causes us to pray for someone. In general, however, this gift commences to operate when by an act of the will, we reach out in faith to God for the information which we require.

# THE WORD OF KNOWLEDGE COMES IN VARIOUS WAYS (1 Corinthians 12:6).

**1.** It comes as DEFINITE IMPRESSIONS conveyed to your spirit by the indwelling Person of the Holy Spirit.

The old Quakers called this, 'the inner witness'. There is a deep settled conviction from within – a strong inner assurance. It is not imagination or guessing or the working of your mind. It has nothing to do with the mind just as speaking in other tongues is not of the mind. God communicates to your spirit – and 'you just know it'. That's all.

**2.** The Word of Knowledge also comes as words from WITHIN, and sometimes as just a single word. It is the blessed privilege of every Christian to be guided and instructed by an INDWELLING VOICE, the voice of the Holy Spirit. When He came in to renew and indwell your spirit the first thing He did was to talk to you. He witnessed to your spirit that you were now a child of God. (Romans 8:16) This, however, was just the beginning. He has come in to talk to you and guide you and instruct you as long as you live. How He talked down in the depths of your heart that time when you were knowingly setting your feet in slippery paths!

Read carefully John 14:26 and John 16:13, 14. Continual communion, fellowship and guidance can be and should be the normal experience of every Christian. In Ezekiel 43:6 we read, "I HEARD SPEAKING TO ME out of the house". You, too, can hear speaking from within the temple which is your body, for within the regenerated man is a center, a speaking voice to which we can 'tune in' and listen. Sometimes from this place of His presence will come floods of great blessings and sometimes there are warnings preparing and calling us to a deeper walk with Christ. Here is "the secret place of the Most High" (Psalm 91:1 KJV) and the soul who finds it abides under the shadow of the Almighty and can hear the voice of the Lord.

But you must LISTEN to Him. Jesus said, "My sheep HEAR MY VOICE" (John 10: 27).

> **"He that hath an ear let him HEAR what the Spirit saith."**
> Revelations 2:7, 17, 29; 3: 13, 22 KJV

**3.** These words from within may be the WORDS OF A SENTENCE giving in the inner man what God is revealing. It sometimes happens that the Word of Knowledge comes in the words of a verse of Scripture. This, however, is not an act of the mind recalling something from memory but an act of the Holy Spirit communicating to your spirit in the language of Scripture the information which you require.

**4.** At various times when praying for the sick I, Tom, have been given strange medical terms which I had never heard before. The sick were healed as I ministered to them according to the Word of Knowledge which God had given me; and later when I consulted a medical dictionary I found the same words.

**5.** Often the Word of Knowledge is something which you SEE as with closed eyes you wait for God's revelation. Then as upon a screen appear letters, words, symbols, scenes, and pictures. God uses these likenesses or "similitudes", as Hosea 12:10 KJV ("visions" in the NIV) calls them, to embody and convey to you the Word of Knowledge which you seek. Note how frequently the word "saw" occurs in Amos 1:1; 7:1-6; 7:8-9; 8:1-2. Note also how each vision was followed by a word of explanation to make clear the meaning. (Compare Daniel 5:24-28). If at any time you do not understand what you are shown, it is quite in order for you to ask for an interpretation (1 Corinthians 14:13) which will usually be given by the voice of the Inner Witness. If, however, no interpretation is forthcoming, go ahead in blind faith ministering according to what has been shown and God will meet with you.

**6.** A clear and distinct VISION, sometimes in color, may appear before you when your eyes are open. This is unusual, however. (Numbers 24:3-4; Acts 12:9; and the Book of Revelation).

**7.** Those who pray for the sick frequently FEEL in their own bodies what is going on in the body of the sick one; and by this particular operation of the Word of Knowledge they can also feel the power of God as it moves in healing virtue into the afflicted body.

**8.** Sometimes an AUDIBLE VOICE is heard but this seldom happens. (1 Samuel 3:4; 9:15; Isaiah 22:14). At such time the voice often seems to come from behind.

**9.** A Word of Knowledge is frequently given as one reads the Bible. The Holy Spirit reveals to your spirit a new and vivid PERSONAL message suited to the need of the hour. WHENEVER we read the Word, our prayer should be, "Lord, SPEAK to me NOW". (Read Psalm 119:19

Now that you have learned some of the ways in which you may expect this gift to operate in your own ministry, you immediately find yourself confronted with the perplexing problem, HOW DO I GET IT TO WORK?

## HOW DO I GET IT TO WORK?

**1.** First of all, close your EYES, shut out everything and shut yourself in with God. Shut out your own desires and anything you may know or think in the matter. Insofar as it is possible, hold your mind blank so that you do not even think.

**2.** Now with all your heart will to know His will. YEARN for it. (See Psalm 119:131). Let your spirit reach out in faith for it. EXPECT THE GIFT TO WORK. Expect God to make it to operate. You are His servant and you want orders so that His business may be done.

**3.** LISTEN WITHIN. God says "Be STILL and know that I am God". (Psalm 46: 10). When He speaks He speaks in stillness, and He reveals His will in the place where He dwells by His Spirit – the throne room of your inner man. You are not concentrating on the problem on hand. You are concentrating on Him, the solver. LISTEN for what God is telling you.

**4**. LOOK WITHIN. When you want to see something in the natural world you open your eyes and start looking. Now, to see in the realm of the spirit you close your eyes and begin to look. Closing your eyes enables you to shut out the distracting things of the world of the senses so that you can concentrate on what God is showing you. Just as in this everyday world you have confidence in the natural ability of human sight so now in the spiritual realm start looking WITH EVEN GREATER CONFIDENCE IN YOUR GOD GIVEN ABILITY OF SPIRITUAL SIGHT. Paul said, "We look at the things which are unseen". (2 Corinthians 4: 18) The Hebrew prophet because of this ability to SEE the things of God was sometimes called a seer.

**5**. If you are praying for the sick, expect to FEEL or sense it in your own body.

If you find it very difficult to enter into the operation of this gift, do these things before you do anything else:

    **A**. Worship and praise either aloud or silently.
    **B**. Assure Him of all your love and devotion.
    **C**. Speak aloud or inaudibly in other tongues.

There is a reason why this will help you. To speak in other tongues you must stir up faith and bring it upon the scene. Now you simply divert this faith into another channel and use it to cause the gift of the Word of Knowledge to operate. The same applies in the operation of the other gifts.

What if you do not receive immediately? Stand your ground.

    **"Though the vision tarry, wait for it."**
    Habakkuk 2:3 KJV

In most cases, however, it is God's will for you to receive now.

## EXCEPTIONS:

1. The need has already been prayed for and God has undertaken.
2. It may be that for certain good reasons of His own, God will not to answer until later. (Jeremiah 42:7).
3. I, Tom, can recall an instance when all I could get was silence because, as I found out later, the situation was such that it was best for me not to get involved in it.
4. Satan or some of his higher powers are turning such pressure upon you that you are distracted and hindered from receiving and ministering. The remedy: Command "the strong man" to be bound in the Name of Jesus.(Mark 3:26, 27; Matthew 18:18).

There are seasons in the Christian life when the going is hard and you are enduring the trial of your faith. (1 Peter 1:6, 7) Suddenly a very real need presents itself, and a Word of Knowledge is essential that you may move and act in the will of God. At such times the witness of the Spirit is sometimes faint – but it is still a witness. That which is revealed is momentary, hazy and indistinct – but you have seen it. You ask for bread – and God has not given you a stone. (Matthew 7: 9, Luke 11: 11) GRASP the revelation such as it is – AND ACT ON IT. I say to you, GOD WILL MEET WITH YOU and will confirm your words and actions.

Often I have acted when there was no time for revelation – and God was gracious. Miracles are not wrought by revelation but by the FAITH of God in ACTION. (You might refer here to Chapter Nine – The Gift of Miracles.)

Let me say for your encouragement that as you go on, faith and confidence will increase and the gift will begin to operate instantly, spontaneously and automatically. You will find yourself speaking it forth. Thus it was that Peter, like a man speaking in other tongues, burst forth with the Word of Knowledge,

> **"Thou art the Christ, the Son of the living God."**
> Matthew 16: 16

Sometimes the coming of the Word of Knowledge is so natural and without effort that for the moment one fails to realize that it is the gift of the Word of Knowledge in operation and not the human mind.

# IMPORTANT – TO MAINTAIN THE OPERATION OF THIS GIFT AND ALL THE GIFTS

To maintain the operation of this gift and all the gifts at a high level, do these things:

Let your own words be few. Commune much with God. Give yourself to prayer. Build up your spiritual strength continually by the Word of God and by speaking much in other tongues. Be full of the Holy Ghost, live in the Spirit, and walk in the Spirit.

# CHAPTER THREE THE GIFT OF DISCERNING OF SPIRITS
## 1 Corinthians 12:10

1. GOD is a SPIRIT. (John 4:24)
2. God's ANGELS are spirits (Hebrews 1:7, 14).
3. SATAN is a spirit. (Ephesians 2:2)
4. The Devil's ANGELS are spirits. (Luke 10:17, 20; 1 Timothy 4:1; Revelations 16:14)
5. MAN is a spirit though clothed in flesh. (Job 32:8; James 2:26; Zechariah 12:1)

The unseen realm of spirits, or the spirit world, extends from Earth to Heaven.

The realm is the "heavenlies" of Ephesians 1:3; 1:20; 2:6; 3:10; 6:12 and John 3:12.

The realm is the "all heavens" of Ephesians 4:10 and constitutes the three heavens – the heaven of the clouds, the heaven of the stars and the heaven which is God's abode.

It is "the air" of Ephesians 2:2, the atmosphere surrounding the earth, a place of intense activity where the unseen Prince and his demons work their will among the human "children of disobedience". (Ephesians 2:2,3; 5:8). Ephesians 6:12 gives us some idea of the immensity and complexity of Satan's empire.

**¹² For our struggle is not against flesh and blood, but against the rulers, against the authorities, against the powers of this dark world and against the spiritual forces of evil in the heavenly realms.**
Ephesians 6:12

Man cannot 'see' in the spirit world except by the power of Satan or by the power of God. There is a Satanic counterfeit, spirits of divination and familiar spirits giving to those who dabble in the occult a certain amount of power to see in the realm of the unseen. There is also the genuine – the gift of God, Discerning of Spirits, which enables Christians to see and discern in the spirit world.

GIFT OF DISCERNING OF SPIRITS IS THE GOD-GIVEN ABILITY TO RECOGNIZE THAT WHICH IS SPIRIT, AND TO KNOW WHAT SPIRIT IT IS.

The ability to detect the presence and identity of a spirit is usually accompanied by an insight into WHAT THE SPIRIT IS DOING. This is important because it puts you in a better position to cope with the situation.

The Greek word used for "discerning" in 1 Corinthians 12:10, has exactly the same meaning as the English word used in our Bible. The dictionary defines this word "discerning" as follows: "power of perception; insight; act or power of seeing clearly."

Hence, discerning of spirits means:

1. POWER OR PERCEPTION of spirits.
2. INSIGHT into the presence and working of spirits.
3. Act or power of SEEING CLEARLY what is going on in the spirit realm.

Man, a powerless prisoner in this world of the senses, is suddenly by the gift of Discerning of Spirits enabled to enter and behold the things of the spirit world which operate the mighty controlling powers both Divine and Satanic. Such was the continual experience of mighty Bible characters, though only a few instances are given. One of these men was Elisha. (See 2 Kings 6:15-17). Another was Micaiah. (Read 2 Chronicles 18:16-22) Paul was another (Concerning his experiences in the realm of the spirit, read Colossians 2:5; 1 Corinthians 5:3; 2 Corinthians 12:1-7)

Such men do not fear the dark lord and his powers. For those who dwell in the secret place of the Most High and are children of His Kingdom of light live at once in two worlds and against seen and unseen, they have great power.

Paul said,

> **"We look not at the things which are seen but at the things which are not seen."**
> 2 Corinthians 4:18 KJV

This in its fullest sense could mean only one thing – an outstanding operation of the gift of Discerning of Spirits. THIS CAN BE YOURS ALSO!

Now, before we continue further, let me point out that this gift is not 'the gift of discernment'. It is the gift of Discerning OF SPIRITS. Furthermore, it is a gift to DISCERN spirits – not to cast them out, which is the work of the gift of Faith and the gift of Miracles.

# BY THIS GIFT WE CAN DISCERN

1. DISCERN THE SPIRIT OF GOD AND THE SPIRITS OF GOD'S ANGELS as they work in the lives of saved and unsaved. (2 Chronicles 18:16-22; 2 Kings 6:15-17; Genesis 32:1-2) Thus we KNOW what God is doing and can take courage.

2. DISCERN THE PRESENCE OF SATAN, AND WHAT HE IS WORKING AGAINST GOD'S LEADERS, against churches, against individuals. This gift is especially imparted to those who shepherd the flock and are WATCHMEN to the house of Israel (Acts 20:29,30; Ezekiel 33:7). Forewarned they can BIND the Strong Man. (Mark 3:26, 27)

3. DISCERN DEMON SPIRITS and their names that they may be cast out.

4. DISCERN THE SPIRIT OF MAN.

Why is it so necessary to discern the working of Satan and his demon spirits? Because otherwise, you are shooting in the dark. With Discerning of Spirits you can pinpoint he target and blast it at will. You can set people free who are being misled, tormented and afflicted in mind and body.

# SATAN AND HIS SPIRITS CAN BE DIVIDED INTO THREE GROUPS

1. Ruling spirits, exalted and powerful, who from their elevated position of authority in the heavenlies directly uphold and control the operation of numerous spirits of subordinate rank. (Ephesians 6:12). These you BIND IN THE NAME OF JESUS when they oppose you or when they attempt to uphold the power of some inferior demon whom you are casting out.

2. Spirits which attack and work through the human mind.

3. Spirits which afflict the human body.

Spirits in classes 2 and 3 can be bound and cast out or can be commanded to go into the Pit if they refuse to obey.

There are other classes of spirits, such as those who work and control in the affairs of the nations, but they are not a matter of direct concern to you.

With this gift of Discerning of Spirits, you can minister to prayer requests from thousands of miles away. You can minister to the needs of people who are not even aware of what you are doing. But the spirits you discern know they hear the word of command across the miles and they must obey it.

As in the operation of the gift of the Word of Knowledge you deliberately WAIT for revelation, EXPECTING to receive it. You may with advantage read again what was written about receiving the Word of Knowledge. What is applicable in the one case is equally applicable in the other.

WHEN IT IS NECESSARY AND IN GOD'S WILL, we may by this gift DISCERN THE SPIRIT OF MAN. This is a matter of "knowing no man according to the flesh" (2 Corinthians 5: 16), of "looking not at the things that are seen, but at the things that are not seen" (2 Corinthians 4: 18). When the prophet Nathan looked at David's brother he fell into the old human error of using his natural MIND. (1 Samuel 16: 6) Then the Lord told him not to look on the outward APPEARANCE but on the SPIRIT of the man. (1 Samuel 16: 7)

Thus it was that by the gift of Discerning of Spirits a man of God CALLED a servant of God to an OFFICE and to a WORK. Paul was similarly guided when in his office of apostle he ordained elders. (Acts 14:23)

This gift is especially useful when you are praying for salvation. YOU KNOW when the seeker has really received Christ into his heart (Acts 8:37). You also know when he has not (Acts 8:9-23). Peter said "I PERCEIVE" (Acts 8: 23) – he was discerning the man's spirit. To lead a man into an assurance of something which he does not possess is no kindness to him, and it certainly is not honoring to God.

How is one shown? There are many ways. I, Tom, am usually shown a lighted candle when the person is a believer. (Proverbs 20:27)

A word of warning is in order here. Such intimate knowledge is revealed for only ONE purpose, that God's work may be advanced or that an individual may be blessed and helped. It is NOT given to gratify curiosity. Nor is it to be used for personal advantage, or to gratify pride and exalt self. It is NOT to be made a subject for gossip among the believers. You are given the revelation to do the job – AND THEN FORGET ABOUT IT! Otherwise you are not ministering gifts in the SUPERNATURAL LOVE of 1 Corinthians 13.

REMEMBER, God sees more failure in ALL of us than any one person could ever see by the gift of Discerning of Spirits – AND YET GOD GOES ON USING US!

This gift detects the SPIRIT OF MAN in prophecy which is not of God and in interpretation which is not right. In Ezekiel 13:2, 3 the Bible speaks of those who "prophesy out of their own hearts – follow their own spirits and have seen nothing".

The gift of Discerning of Spirits is the EYES of the Church. Without it, the church cannot see and cope with powers of hell tearing it apart by strife and confusion. Without it, the church cannot tell what spiritual manifestations in the service are of God and what are of other origin.

# CHAPTER FOUR
# THE GIFT OF TONGUES
# 1 Corinthians 12:10

There is speaking in other tongues, which is A SIGN and there is speaking in other tongues, which is A GIFT. When it first occurs, speaking in other tongues is a sign that the believer has just been filled with the Holy Spirit; thereafter it continues in the believer's ministry as one of the nine gifts of the Spirit.

In its three aspects tongues is:

1. A SIGN TO UNBELIEVERS
2. A SIGN TO BELIEVERS
3. A GIFT OF THE HOLY SPIRIT

Tongues, as an evidence of the supernatural working of God, was a sign to unbelievers on the day of Pentecost. (Acts 2:11)

Jesus said in Mark 16:17 KJV:

> **"These SIGNS shall follow them that believe ... they shall speak with new tongues."**

The Apostle Paul, quoting Isaiah 28: 11-12 KJV:

> **"With men of other tongues and other lips will I speak to this people"**

Then he adds,

> "**Wherefore tongues are for a SIGN not to them that believe but for them that believe not.**"
> 1 Corinthians 14:21, 22 KJV

But tongues is also AN EVIDENCE to the believer that God has just filled with the Holy Spirit. Jesus had said to the disciples,

> "**Tarry ye ... until ye be endued with power from on high.**"
> Luke 24:49 KJV

Then on the day of Pentecost when the disciples had all spoken simultaneously in other tongues, Peter by way of explanation declared,

> "**God hath shed forth this (the gift of the Holy Ghost) which you now SEE and HEAR**"
> Acts 2:33 KJV

It is apparent from Acts 10: 45-46 that tongues is THE SIGN and EVIDENCE of the baptism of the HOLY GHOST.

> [45] **The circumcised believers who had come with Peter were astonished that the gift of the Holy Spirit had been poured out even on Gentiles.** [46] **For they heard them speaking in tongues and praising God.**
> Acts 10:45-46

In this course, however, we must mainly concern ourselves with tongues as one of the gifts of the Spirit.

THE GIFT OF TONGUES IS THE GOD GIVEN ABILITY WHICH ENABLES A BELIEVER TO SPEAK AT WILL IN A LANGUAGE WHICH HE DOES NOT KNOW.

Note that the word "tongues" is in the plural in 1 Cor. 12:10 and 14:18. The gift of tongues is not the ability to speak one language but many.

Sometimes God uses a message in tongues to convey a message to someone present. To him it is not a message in tongues, but a prophecy in his own language.

When tongues was a sign on the Day of Pentecost, they all spoke simultaneously and there was no interpretation of what was said (Acts 2). In the congregation, however, when edification is the object, two or three are to exercise the gift each IN HIS TURN and to be in Divine order there MUST be interpretation after each message in tongues. (1 Cor. 14: 27) If you do not as yet interpret and you know that there is no one present to interpret then do not give a message in tongues. Paul is not trying to hinder the moving of the Spirit in services but is suggesting that due order and balance be kept in mind. Have you ever noticed, three interpretations and three prophecies will IN GENERAL provide the right proportion of inspired utterance for MOST services.

The purpose of the gift of tongues is TO EDIFY THE CHURCH when accompanied by interpretation and TO EDIFY THE INDIVIDUAL CHRISTIAN when he speaks in tongues in his private devotions.

To edify means "to build up, to strengthen". It is your

spirit which is edified. Paul desired above all things that we might "be strengthened WITH MIGHT by His Spirit IN THE INNER MAN". (Ephesians 3:16 KJV) Speaking much in tongues will do this. We know that the Word of His Grace, the written Word will build us up (Acts 20:32), but too many neglect to make use of this other means of edification, speaking in tongues.

NOTE ESPECIALLY THE EMPHASIS WHICH THE BIBLE PLACES ON THE SPIRIT OF MAN IN THIS MATTER OF SPEAKING IN TONGUES.

# WHEN I EXERCISE THE GIFT OF TONGUES:

1. MY SPIRIT IS EDIFIED. (1 Corinthians 14:4). The word edified, or built up, conveys with it the thought of being enlightened, thrilled, blessed, encouraged, strengthened, developed and caused to grow up and mature.

2. MY SPIRIT COMMUNES and has fellowship with God. "In the spirit (His Spirit joined to my spirit) I speak mysteries" (or "Divine secrets", as the Weymouth translation renders it) (1 Corinthians 14:2). Thus are "the deep things of God" revealed to the spirit of man, explaining spiritual realities with Spirit-taught words, not to his understanding only. (1 Corinthians 2:10-16).

3. MY SPIRIT PRAYS and, most important of all, prays

ACCORDING TO THE WILL OF GOD. (1 Corinthians 14:14,15; also read Romans 8:26,27) I can pray with the understanding and sometimes not receive because I am not asking according to the will of God, but when I pray in another tongue I am ALWAYS asking in the will of God. To pray thus is to always receive. Read 1 John 5:14, 15. Moreover, when my spirit prays in tongues the Holy Ghost causes me to pray for THINGS WHICH OUGHT TO BE PRAYED FOR but which no one thinks to pray for or knows about. Thus needs known only to God are taken care of. The Bible calls this kind of praying "supplication in the Spirit" (Ephesians 6:18 KJV) and "praying in the Holy Ghost"(Jude 1:20).

Tongues is a form of prayer and a much neglected one. Tongues is a way to pray when the mind is perplexed.

**4.** MY SPIRIT WORSHIPS (John 4:23, 24 and Philippians 3:3). Here is true worship in spirit and in truth, the kind of worship which God seeks for.

**5.** When in the midst of Satanic opposition I speak in other tongues, the Holy Spirit somehow causes MY SPIRIT to be projected in its influence right into the unseen world where the real conflict is going on. Instead of being a distant spectator one seems to be an actual participant enforcing the victory of Calvary on the enemy.

The weapon of victory is the Sword of the Spirit, the word of God going forth from the mouth whether in a known or in an unknown tongue. These were the kind of conflicts with which Paul was familiar. (Ephesians 6:10-18; 2 Corinthians 10:3-5; Colossians 2:1).

6. MY SPIRIT GIVES THANKS to God in another language and, according to 1 Corinthians 14:17, "gives thanks well."

7. The gift of tongues enables MY SPIRIT TO SING IN OTHER TONGUES unto the Lord (1 Corinthians 14:15). Sometimes the Spirit of God moves upon an entire congregation and the people break forth into singing in the Spirit like a great heavenly choir, some in English, some in other tongues, and all in perfect harmony. The blessing upon all and the sense of the presence of God is tremendous at such times. May I, Tom, add that apart from God such a thing is unexplainable and wholly IMPOSSIBLE.

8. MY SPIRIT WILLS the instant operation of the gift. By an act of my will I CAN SPEAK IN OTHER TONGUES AT ANY TIME. This is in agreement with 1 Corinthians 14:15 KJV: "I WILL pray with the spirit AND WILL PRAY with the understanding also." Because this gift can be brought into operation at will, the believer can avail himself of needed help without delay. Speaking in tongues is the most important thing one can do to feed, build up and strengthen the spirit. It is a 'QUICK CHARGE' of gigantic power and permanent benefit. It "STRENGTHENS WITH MIGHT IN THE INNER MAN" (Ephesians 3: 16 KJV). Paul that spiritual stalwart said:

> **"I thank God I speak in tongues more than ye all."**
> 1 Corinthians 14:18 KJV

9. There is some relation between the well-being of the spirit and the well-being of the body. (3 John 2). "A joyful heart (spirit) doeth good like a medicine"

(Proverbs 17: 22 KJV). I have many times observed that the practice of speaking in tongues which builds up and strengthens the spirit has at the same time the effect of giving new life to the body. Faith is built up and released so that the Holy Spirit has greater liberty to move throughout the mortal body and quicken it. (Romans 8:11)

If you do not speak in tongues in your daily prayer life it indicates that:

a) You do not really appreciate THE VALUE of it.
b) Or else, you do not understand how this gift operates. Realize this: God does not do the speaking, YOU DO THE SPEAKING. In Acts 2:4 we read "ALL OF THEM were filled with the Holy Spirit and began to speak in other tongues as the Spirit enabled them."

If you do not find it easy to speak in other tongues, first throw yourself with ENERGY into praising God in a LOUD VOICE. Then commence to speak in tongues.

To stir up the other gifts of the Spirit within you, throw yourself with energy and emphasis into speaking in another tongue. GIVE YOURSELF WHOLLY TO SPEAKING. The more intense the giving the greater will be the power and blessing and revelation of the Spirit within you and the more effective will be the operation of the other gifts. By speaking in other tongues you move more readily into the realm of the Spirit.

Sometimes when you are praying for the sick and afflicted, you find that you have come against some stubborn thing that will not move. Minister in tongues, for tongues is the bridge into the unseen world where most Satanic hindrances and opposition are entrenched. As you speak, you enter in more fully and overcome by the sword of the Spirit.

Some will ask, "When people speak in tongues, do they speak in REAL LANGUAGES?"

Yes, on the Day of Pentecost, they spoke in real languages (Acts 2:4-6) and the same thing takes place today. Read *They Speak With Other Tongues* by John Sherrill[2] (John Lewis Sherrill 1923-2017). I may add that as the result of personal observation and experience and also because of the reliable testimony of ministers, missionaries and laymen whom I, Tom, have known, I have no alternative than to believe that the languages spoken are real languages and that in certain cases these languages have been used to proclaim the Gospel.

# CHAPTER FIVE
# THE GIFT OF INTERPRETATION OF TONGUES
# 1 Corinthians 12:10

THE GIFT OF INTERPRETATION OF TONGUES IS THE GOD-GIVEN ABILITY TO BRING FORTH IN A LANGUAGE KNOWN TO THE SPEAKER THE INTERPRETATION OF AN UNKNOWN MESSAGE GIVEN PREVIOUSLY BY THE GIFT OF TONGUES.

The interpretation may be a word-for-word translation. More often it is a message giving THE SENSE of that which has been spoken by the Gift of Tongues. In the latter case the interpretation may be either longer or shorter than the message in tongues. (This is in harmony with Daniel 5:24-28 where Daniel was asked by King Belshazzar to interpret the four words mene, mene, tekel and parse.)

Interpretation, like prophecy, is entirely INSPIRATIONAL and SUPERNATURAL in its operation. For this reason it would be profitable to read the part of the course dealing with the Gift of Prophecy. YOU DO NOT KNOW BEFOREHAND what you are going to say. As you give the interpretation it is as new to you as to those who hear it.

If you already speak in tongues, then you are to ask God to give you the Gift of Interpretation also. (1 Corinthians 14:13) It is perfectly in order to interpret your own message in tongues; it is also in order for you to interpret the message of another. If you know that there is no one in the church capable of giving interpretation and if you yourself do not interpret, then YOU MUST NOT give a message in tongues. Instead you may speak to yourself and to God. (1 Corinthians 14:28)

Some do not esteem tongues with interpretation as highly as prophecy, while others will tell you that tongues plus interpretation is in a sense GREATER than prophecy for the reason that there are two supernatural gifts in operation instead of one.

If you are giving messages in other tongues, obey the Word and ask God for interpretation; request prayer if necessary, and COMMENCE to give interpretation.

Remember, THE ABILITY TO DO SO IS ALREADY WITHIN YOU.

# CHAPTER SIX
# THE GIFT OF PROPHECY
# 1 Corinthians 12:10

According to the Word of God,

> **"he that prophesieth speaking unto men to edification, and exhortation, and comfort."**
> 1 Corinthians 14:3 KJV

> Edification: *building up*
> Exhortation: *encouraging*
> Comfort: *consoling*

Or, as Ellicott, (Charles John Ellicott D.D., 1819–1905)[3] aptly termed it: "Building up, stirring up, cheering up."

IT IS SPEAKING AS GOD'S MOUTHPIECE, according to 1 Peter 4:11. John the Baptist, the last of the Old Testament prophets was called "A Voice Proclaiming".

The Greek language in which the New Testament was originally written has one word for prophecy and its meaning is "TO SPEAK FOR ANOTHER".

The Hebrew has three words for the word 'prophecy' and they give a beautiful picture of this wonderful gift in operation:

1. To bubble forth, spring forth (as a spring).
2. To let drop (as rain from Heaven).
3. To lift up (uplift).

THE GIFT OF PROPHECY IS THE GOD-GIVEN ABILITY TO SPEAK FORTH A MESSAGE FROM GOD, WHICH YOU ARE RECEIVING BY INSPIRATION AS YOU ARE GIVING IT FORTH.

It is entirely inspirational and is just as new to the one who gives it as to those who hear it. It is NOT something which you prepared and had in mind previously and then gave when you came into the church. 2 Peter 1:21 KJV tells us that

> **"prophecy came not by the will of man but holy men of God spake as they were moved by the Holy Ghost."**

YOU do the speaking, but you speak AS YOU ARE MOVED BY THE HOLY SPIRIT. You do not guide or control what is coming from your tongue. Even Balaam, a prophet who loved money, said,

> **"Have I any power at all to say anything? The word that God putteth in MY MOUTH, that shall I speak."**
> Numbers 22: 38 KJV

Prophecy proceeds not from the mind but from the mouth.

Can prophecy be controlled and directed by the one who gives it? Yes, but this according to the Scripture definition is not true prophecy.

The one who thus presumes to bring forth something which is of his own manufacture is not sinning in ignorance; HE INVARIABLY IS AWARE OF WHAT

HE IS DOING – at least in the beginning. Later on, a deceiving spirit is apt to enter into his prophesying and he may be so misled that he will actually believe that what he brings forth is of God.

A believer who is cherishing a root of bitterness is in danger of going off into false prophecy. HE MAY NOT, but the possibility is there because he is defiled. If a man is permitting the enemy to influence or control him in any way this will eventually, to a greater or lesser degree, be reflected in his testifying, his teaching, his preaching and his ministry. In general and also there will be defilement in the spiritual gifts which are an important part of his ministry.

In other words, there are times when prophecy can be wrong, and this is the reason why the Bible says that PROPHECY is to be judged, that is, spiritually discerned or examined. (1 Corinthians 14:29-33). Naturally, the ones who are to do this are those who are competent to do so – the prophets, and those with the gift of Discerning of Spirits.

But because some prophecy can be uninspired, let not God's people become alarmed or take lightly THIS GREAT GIFT which God has given TO BUILD UP BELIEVERS. Paul, in 1 Thessalonians 5:19-21 KJV clearly outlines what our attitude should be regarding prophecy:

**"Quench not the Spirit".**

Prophesy, and permit others to prophesy.

**"Despise not prophesyings".**

Literally, DISREGARD NOT prophesyings.

**"Prove all things".**

Judge prophecy.

**"HOLD FAST THAT WHICH IS GOOD".**

For the encouragement of sincere believers WHO ARE AFRAID OF BRING FORTH SOMETHING WRONG when they prophesy, I, Tom, have this to say: BECAUSE you are concerned, God will not let you prophesy anything but His word. I have proven this fact thousands of times – that you can rely upon the truth and accuracy of prophecy.

Someone has expressed it thus: "Prophecy is INFALLIBLE to the extent that the channel of prophecy is YIELDED TO GOD".

We must, however, realize that when a person FIRST BEGINS to give messages in prophecy, he sometimes unconsciously permits his own mind to enter into what he is bringing forth, with the result that what he says is party inspired and partly not. This is not something to cause grave concern. His heart is right, and soon, like the beginner riding a bicycle, he finds himself naturally and easily continuing along the course which he should follow.

Sometimes the beginner is discouraged because the prophecy he brings forth is SIMPLE and rather LACKING IN DEPTH. May I point out that the great river and the little stream have the SAME SOURCE, the SAME WATER, and both have MORE

THAN ENOUGH WATER to supply the needs of a thirsty man. BOTH ARE CHANNELS OF LIFE AND REFRESHING. The only difference is that the one channel has greater depth than the other. As we go on, God deepens us and deepens our capacity to minister.

The Gift of Prophecy is for all (1 Corinthians 14:5 and 31) and Paul was concerned that all the believers should have it.

In 1 Corinthians 14:29 Paul suggests that two or three prophecies by those who are PROPHETS is enough. In the case of others who merely have the GIFT of prophecy, it would seem from verse 24 that Paul did not set a limit, though the general rule concerning order and good taste would apply here also. See verse 40.

# THOSE WHO BENEFIT FROM PROPHECY

"Prophecy serveth for **(1** THEM WHICH BELIEVE" (1 Corinthians 14:22 KJV). It is to edify, exhort, comfort and teach (1 Corinthians 14:3 KJV). Note that the King James Version also uses the word "learn" (1 Corinthians 14:31 KJV).

Prophecy is also for **(2** THE UNBELIEVER and **(3** the UNLEARNED (the immature believer) to "convince" him by revealing the secrets of his heart. (1 Corinthians 14:24, 25)

# PROPORTION OF FAITH

YOU PROPHECY ACCORDING TO THE PROPORTION OF FAITH (Romans 12:6).

Dictionary: 'Proportion': equal or just share.

The PROPORTION OF FAITH is called in verse 3 the measure of faith.

NOTE, this measure of faith, this share of faith which is yours is not according to what man can do or is capable of. It is ACCORDING TO WHAT GOD HAS BESTOWED UPON US!

> **"His power to us-ward is ACCORDING to the working of HIS MIGHTY POWER which he wrought in Christ when ..."**
> Ephesians 1:19-21 KJV

This faith, this power is according to the infinite resources which he has already deposited to our account to write cheques against!

So when you prophecy, launch out boldly into the deep. Prophecy according to your share of faith, which is more than you can ever reach the limits of.

The scope of prophecy is infinite. It reaches out and covers and past, the present and the future.

PROPHECY IS THE TESTIMONY OF JESUS for, according to Revelations 19:10:

> **"The testimony of Jesus is the Spirit of prophecy."**

The 'Spirit of Jesus' was in the Old Testament prophets just as He is in us (1 Peter 1:11). Therefore, PROPHECY is JESUS SPEAKING HIS wonderful words in the midst of the congregation.

# SOME OF THE THINGS THAT PROPHECY IS NOT:

1. Prophecy is NOT PREACHING, nor is it "inspired preaching" as some modern Bible translators have knowingly and incorrectly rendered the word.

2. Prophecy is not an opportunity to scold the believer. Neither is prophecy a way of telling someone in public what you ought to have the courage to tell him privately. Prophecy is not something which comes by the will and direction of man but something which you speak as you are moved by the Holy Spirit.

3. Prophecy does not consist of repeating a message that you have given many times before in previous meetings.

The gift of prophecy does not make a man a prophet. All prophets have the gift of prophecy, but all having the gift of prophecy are not prophets.

1 Corinthians 14:31 KJV says:

**"For ye may ALL prophecy, that all may learn."**

Therefore, THE GIFT is for all believers.

But the prophetic OFFICE or ministry is not for all, for 1 Corinthians 12:28, 29, asks the question, "Are all prophets?" No, all are not prophets as this verse clearly indicates. The office of a prophet is a MINISTERIAL GIFT (1 Corinthians 12: 28, 29; Ephesians 3:5 and 4:11).

Prophetic utterances of a prophet are usually deeper and more apt to be predictive.

In the New Testament we find the test of prophecy given in 1 John 4:1-3. You challenge the evil spirit to answer your question, and thereby reveal his presence. "Spirit, in the Name of Jesus I command you to answer: DID JESUS CHRIST COME IN THE FLESH?" An answer in the negative always indicates that the prophecy was demonically inspired.

When the gift of Discerning of Spirits is present, it is not necessary to use this method.

# CHAPTER SEVEN
# THE GIFT OF FAITH
# 1 Corinthians 12:9

Faith, the power or ability to believe, is the greatest ability that we can possess. It is a golden key.

> **"Without faith it is impossible to please God"**
> Hebrews 11:6 KJV

> **"but ALL THINGS are possible to him that believeth."**
> Mark 9:23 KJV

## THREE KINDS OF FAITH

There are three kinds of faith and all three are the gift of God. (Ephesians 2:8)

1. There is the faith which God gives us in order that we can believe and be saved. This faith is the power given us by God to receive Jesus as our Savior and so become sons of God. (John 1:12). We may call it SAVING FAITH.
2. There is also the faith which is A FRUIT OF THE SPIRIT, a steadfast and ever increasing confidence in God which with the other fruits of the Spirit constitutes mature Christian character (Galatians. 5:22).

3. Greatest of all is the GIFT OF FAITH mentioned in 1 Corinthians 12:9. THIS IS SPECIAL FAITH, ATOMIC FAITH, FAITH TO WORK MIRACLES. A single grain of it though small as a mustard seed has power to overturn a mountain. (Matthew 17:20) If you have been filled with the Holy Spirit, the gift of faith is within you whether you realize the fact or not, for this gift, like its companion gifts, resides in and is a manifestation of the indwelling Holy Spirit. And whether the gift of faith is to operate in your ministry or not, depends entirely on YOU, for Jesus said,

**"HAVE the faith of God".**

(In the original Greek this is the actual wording of Mark 11:22, and this passage is thus rendered in the marginal readings of various Bibles as well as in the Revised Version.)

# FAITH OF GOD EXAMINED

Let us closely examine Mark 11:21 - 23 and see what the FAITH OF GOD really is.

1. It is GOD'S faith, the faith which God himself has – that Divine confidence in all that He says, in all that He does. God does not wonder or doubt in His heart!

2. It is the faith which is IRRESISTIBLE – THE FAITH WHICH COMMANDS AND IT IS DONE.

3. It is the faith which God GIVES TO YOU – which HE COMMANDS you to have: "HAVE THE FAITH OF GOD". Because your faith would not avail, God gives you His faith.

4. The possessor of THIS faith need not doubt – HE BELIEVES that WHAT HE SAYS WILL COME TO PASS.

YOU ARE USING GOD'S IRRESISTIBLE FAITH TO SPEAK GOD'S IRRESISTIBLE WORDS THAT GOD'S IRRESISTIBLE POWER MAY BE RELEASED.

Meditate upon it, repeat it, shout it – this is your heritage.

THE GIFT OF FAITH IS THE GOD GIVEN ABILITY TO BELIEVE GOD FOR THE IMPOSSIBLE.

The gift of God's faith is a spiritual ability which YOU operate just as you would any natural ability which you can use at will. When the believer maintains a close daily walk with God, and is full of the Spirit at all times, this gift is almost spontaneous in its working. Just as a sudden drop in temperature causes the thermostat to turn on the heat, so the utter hopelessness of a situation, the awful reality of inescapable danger and death, the towering mountain of impossibility blocking your pathway, all CAUSE THE GIFT OF FAITH TO SOAR VICTORIOUSLY, AND YOU BELIEVE GOD FOR THE FANTASTICALLY IMPOSSIBLE. This gift causes perfect peace and confidence to reign in the heart and MAKES GOD'S SERVANT MASTER OF THE SITUATION no matter how dangerous it may be. Read the story of the untroubled prophet in 2 Kings 6:32-7:2. Also read Hebrews 11.

The gift of faith will cause the other gifts to operate in greater power and fullness. This is especially so when the gift of faith ministers the gift of miracles, the two gifts working in combination (Acts 6:8). You are then multiplying the power, using a gift of power to minister a gift of power.

Many do not realize that a person with the gift of faith can IMPART FAITH to others. By the faith of God you are speaking WORDS OF FAITH which in turn PRODUCE FAITH.

THE GIFT OF FAITH IS A FAITH WHICH LAYS HOLD AND COMMANDS. You can confidently say, "ACCORDING TO THE FAITH OF GOD IN MY HEART, WHICH CANNOT DOUBT, I command it done."

How can one cause this wonderful God given ability to be mighty in its operation? BY HEARING THE WORD OF THE LORD.

# FAITH COMETH BY HEARING THE WORD OF GOD

"Faith cometh by hearing the word of God".
Romans 10:17 KJV

1. God speaks to you when you read the Bible, and faith comes by hearing His word. You should read and study the Bible continually.

2. God speaks to you in a dream or in a vision or by one of the revelation gifts, and faith comes because you have heard His word.

3. Also, though you may not have thought of it in this way, you hear the word of the Lord WHEN YOU ARE SPEAKING ALOUD IN OTHER TONGUES. The sound goes into your ears and the Bible says that you are BUILT UP IN YOUR SPIRIT even though your mind understands it not. (1 Corinthians 14:4) Faith has come by the hearing of His Word.

4. To receive quickly and in concentrated measure do what I frequently do – walk up and down with your open Bible in your hand and repeat over and over for minutes at a time one of the FAITH-BUILDING, MIRACLE-INSPIRING PASSAGES which abound in the Scriptures; continue until the fulness of the passage has SATURATED you; then pass on to another portion and repeat in the same manner; and speak in a loud voice so that the room

and your ears and your mind are filled and resounding with the power and the Spirit and the majesty of the IRRESISTIBLE WORDS OF THE LORD.

Use every means at your disposal, my brother, to MAINTAIN MIGHTY MIRACLE-WORKING FAITH.

# CHAPTER EIGHT
# GIFTS OF HEALING
# 1 Corinthians 12:9

Satan is the ORIGINATOR of sickness and death (Gen 2:17 and 3:1-19; Romans 5:12). In Acts 10:38 KJV, we read,

> **"Jesus ... went about ... healing ALL THAT WERE OPPRESSED OF THE DEVIL."**

Every sickness, deformity and disease on earth was and is the result of Satan's work. Christ came to heal, cure and restore.

Satan is the PROPAGATOR of sickness (Luke 13:11-16). His work is carried out through certain evil spirits who specialize in afflicting humanity either directly or indirectly. For example, there are "spirits of infirmity" (sickness) which cause sickness and disease in the body. The woman in Luke 13:11 had been afflicted by such a spirit. There are also spirits which cause deafness, dumbness and epilepsy (Mark 9:14-27), unclean or lewd spirits which enter the mind to control and pollute it (Mark 1:23), psychic spirits of divination which enable people to foretell future events (Acts 16:16), lying spirits (2 Chronicles 18:22), religious spirits, spirits of insanity, homosexual spirits[4], spirits which incite to violence, suicide and murder, spirits of adultery and lust, spirits of nicotine, drugs and of drunkenness. The list is almost endless.

These spirits – also known as demons, are the angels which sinned in the beginning, were cast out of Heaven and are now "the Devil's angels" (Matthew 25:41). Their chains are chains of darkness. They have no godly knowledge and no capacity for heavenly things. Without its heavenly body, spiritual illumination and balance, the demon is a miserable disenfranchised, homeless, psychopathic creature - a strange, abnormal personality of evil. These spirits, who have lost their heavenly bodies, now seek embodiment in human form (Matthew 12:43-45) and in this way, they can work against God.

When demons enter the mind or the body of a human being, they strive to do two things: first to make the individual what they are and second, to satisfy their lusts through him or her. The individual then takes on and expresses the personality of the demon which influences them.

# STAGES OF DEMONIC INFLUENCE

There are three stages of demonic influence:

1. OPPRESSION: the demon works from the outside by throwing thoughts at the mind or by causing pains and symptoms in the body.

2. INFILTRATION: The demon enters the mind and

causes hallucinations, fixations or obsessions. For example, the demon may enter the body and sow a seed of cancer or some other ailment.

3. POSSESSION: In the case of the unsaved person, the demon enters and possesses the darkened, alienated spirit of the sinner. The renewed spirit of the believer has ALREADY been possessed by the Holy Spirit who has come to abide there. If, however, a believer goes deeply into sin, the devil may move into the mind and take full control. Tom found that the same thing can happen to a good Christian who suffers a severe nervous breakdown. Because of bodily weakness they find it impossible for the time being to keep the Enemy out of their mind. In both cases full deliverance can be ministered in the Name of Jesus.

# HEALING IN THE ATONEMENT

The basis – THE GREAT ROCK FOUNDATION for all things pertaining to our full deliverance and complete salvation is CHRIST – Christ, suffering and crucified that through His death he might deliver us from sin, sickness and Satan (Hebrews 2:14, 15). To know that bodily healing is in the Atonement, just as salvation is in the atonement, gives us GREAT ASSURANCE of faith in claiming OUR RIGHTS in Him.

The Bible says Jesus has BORNE our sin and our iniquities (Isaiah 53: 10 - 12).

The Bible says Jesus has BORNE (same Hebrew word) our griefs and our sorrows (that is, "our sicknesses and our pains" -- as Young's translation renders it).

> **4 Surely he took up our pain and bore our suffering, yet we considered him punished by God, stricken by him, and afflicted. 5 But he was pierced for our transgressions, he was crushed for our iniquities; the punishment that brought us peace was on him, and by his wounds we are healed. He bore them both, and at the same time.**
> Isaiah 53:4-5

Furthermore, it was the Holy Spirit who caused Matthew to quote Isaiah 53:4 and apply it to the healing of bodily sicknesses. (Matthew 8:16-17 KJV). We read:

> **16 When the even was come, they brought unto him many that were possessed with devils: and he cast out the spirits with his word, and healed all that were sick:**
>
> **17 THAT IT MIGHT BE FULFILLED which was spoken by Isaiah the prophet, saying, Himself took our infirmities, and bare our sicknesses.**
> Matthew 8:16-17 KJV

*He bore both, and bore them both at the same time.*

Peter also speaks of the same two things – your sins borne in Jesus body on the cross, your sicknesses healed because His body was bruised and broken for you. (1 Peter 2:24).

> **24 "He himself bore our sins" in his body on the cross, so that we might die to sins and live for righteousness; "by his wounds you have been healed."**
> 1 Peter 2:24

# METHODS OF DIVINE HEALING

Because of what Christ has wrought on our behalf there are four methods of healing available to believers.

1. RECOGNITION: Recognizing the fact that healing for the body has been bought and paid for just as salvation has been bought and paid for – you claim God's promise, believe it in your heart and confess it with your mouth. On the basis of what Christ has eternally deposited to our account at Calvary you claim and accept your healing from God just as you claimed and accepted your salvation. If you will believe God for your healing just as you believed God for your salvation, all the powers of hell cannot cheat you out of it.

2. PRAYER OF THE ELDERS: Perhaps you feel too sick to believe or your faith is discouraged and weak. James 5:14-15 outlines a method of deliverance; you merely make the request for help.

> **[14] Is anyone among you sick? Let them call the elders of the church to pray over them and anoint them with oil in the name of the Lord. [15] And the prayer offered in faith will make the sick person well; the Lord will raise them up. If they have sinned, they will be forgiven.**
> James 5:14-15

The elders are the ones who must pray the prayer of faith. They also anoint you with oil – a symbolic act to signify that they are PUTTING THE HOLY SPIRIT UPON YOUR BODY to do the work. Note that the word "any" in James 5 is just as comprehensive in its meaning as the word "whosoever" in John 3:16 and Matthew 8:16. Remember that Acts 5:16 tell us that "all" were healed.

3. CONTACT OBJECTS: Another method is to be found in Acts 19:11-12.

> **[11] God did extraordinary miracles through Paul, [12] so that even handkerchiefs and aprons that had touched him were taken to the sick, and their illnesses were cured and the evil spirits left them.**
> Acts 19:11-12

Great numbers have been miraculously healed in this manner.

4. GIFTS OF HEALING: The gift of healing is one of the nine gifts of the Holy Spirit.

Note that the plural, "gifts" is used. The reason for this is obvious. EVERY healing, just like salvation, is A GIFT – an individual act of God's GRACE – TO YOU! Thus, the promise is sure to all (Romans 4:16).

A GIFT OF HEALING IS THE GOD GIVEN ABILITY TO IMPART HEALING TO ANOTHER IN THE NAME OF JESUS.

> A. The gift is YOURS. Peter said,
>
> > **"WHAT I HAVE that give I ..."**
> > Acts 3: 6 KJV.

B. YOU operate it. Jesus commanded US to heal the sick (Luke 9:1-2 and Mark 16:15-18).

> **[1] When Jesus had called the Twelve together, he gave them power and authority to drive out all demons and to cure diseases, [2] and he sent them out to proclaim the kingdom of God and to heal the sick.**
> Luke 9:1-2 KJV

> **[15] And he said unto them, Go ye into all the world, and preach the gospel to every creature. [16] He that believeth and is baptized shall be saved; but he that believeth not shall be damned. [17] And these signs shall follow them that believe; In my name shall they cast out devils; they shall speak with new tongues; [18] They shall take up serpents; and if they drink any deadly thing, it shall not hurt them; they shall lay hands on the sick, and they shall recover.**
> Mark 16:15-18 KJV

C. You are ABLE to operate it.

> **You minister the ABILITY which God giveth.**
> 1 Peter 4: 11 KJV

> **According to His working which worketh in you mightily.**
> Colossians 1: 29 KJV

The gift of healing in its highest and most effective form operates in conjunction with one or more of the other eight gifts. Let us go from step to step in just such a case.

# STORY OF MR. X

Mr. X is a sick man and you as God's servant are to minister a gift of healing to him. You may feel led of God to pray briefly that He will overshadow and bless all that is said and done unto His Glory or you may find yourself quoting in the Spirit certain appropriate passages of Scripture which would minister faith, or both, or neither, depending on how you feel impressed by the Spirit. It is ALWAYS advisable to close your eyes and wait on the Lord that He may guide you in your praying by A WORD OF KNOWLEDGE. God may show you that there is a spiritual need which must first be taken care of. The GIFT OF DISCERNING OF SPIRITS may show you certain spirits which are afflicting the SPIRIT of Mr. X. He may be sick in his spirit and the enemy is using his spirit as an avenue to attack his physical body. Spirits of fear, confusion, accusing spirits or lying spirits may be telling him that his case is hopeless; this must be revealed and cast out before he can be healed. While in prayer you may be shown personal matters or past sins and actions which constitute the power of the enemy to afflict, and these must be removed once and for all. This is where the GIFT OF THE WORD OF WISDOM comes in. You need the wisdom of God to bring certain facts to Mr. X to help him, and you say it in the love of 1 Corinthians 13. If in a public meeting, you may have the people sing a hymn, so that what you tell Mr. X is heard by no one else.

Sometimes in the case of a discouraged Christian, God will cause you to bring forth a message in TONGUES with INTERPRETATION or else a message in PROPHECY.

Now having dealt with spiritual troubles, you can go on to physical ailments. Here again the WORD OF KNOWLEDGE will direct you in praying and in speaking the word of command. The advantages of hearing the Word of Knowledge are twofold: **(1)** Faith comes to all concerned by hearing the word of God (Romans 10: 17) and **(2)** You are aiming at the mark – ministering to the CAUSE of the trouble and not the result of it, as might otherwise be the case.

Perhaps a physical ailment is the result of some spirit power working in the body. By the gift of DISCERNING OF SPIRITS its presence and identity are revealed, and by the operation of the gift of MIRACLES it is cast out.

For example, perhaps a hopelessly injured spine needs to be restored. By the word of KNOWLEDGE you see the extent and nature of the injury. In Jesus Name you command that which should not exist to vanish away; that which should be, you command to come into existence – and it does. Then you command the vertebrae to come into proper alignment and be held in place by the power of God. The spine obeys, and by the same WORD OF KNOWLEDGE you see it perfect. Here we have the GIFT OF FAITH WORKING IN CONJUNCTION WITH THE GIFT OF MIRACLES that there may be full deliverance.

Before you leave Mr. X get the assurance of the Spirit that there is nothing further to pray for. This information will usually come as a Word of Knowledge.

Usually the needs are not so many and varied in any one individual as in the story of Mr. X. I, Tom, have, however, ministered healing to such cases where the whole nine gifts were in operation.

So far as we can ascertain from the Scriptures, from our observation of facts, and from personal revelation on the subject, these demons, tormentors and destroyers of the human race, range from powerful, violent spirits to a lower rank of less powerful spirits causing less fatal sicknesses. Spirits of murder, insanity, epilepsy, and of cancer are numbered among the powerful ones.

ALWAYS bind the spirit of epilepsy in the Name of Jesus before you cast him out. Otherwise he may immediately enter some other person, fearful or weak in faith, who is standing by. Then you will have to do the job twice. He is one of the most powerful demons (Mark 9:14-27) but he has to obey. ALWAYS ask God to show you what weakness in the natural defenses of the body provided an opening for the epileptic spirit. The usual cause is some pressure on the brain, the result of injury, malformation or brain tumor. This must be ministered to and healed before you can consider the case closed. If not, another similar spirit will enter in and carry on the work.

Malignant cancer is a spirit and a powerful one. This spirit is usually accompanied by the spirit of fear which opens the door for the entry of cancer and also makes the casting out of cancer more difficult. Nevertheless, YOU "have power against unclean spirits to cast them out" (Matthew 10: 1) as you call him by name and command him in the Name of Jesus to leave, he has to obey. Now you must deal with the growth or tumor which the spirit of cancer has caused to form in the body. You are reminded of the results of Jesus cursing the fig tree:

> **Peter remembered and said to Jesus, "Rabbi, look! The fig tree you cursed has withered!"**
> Mark 11:21

Like this the cancer must be cursed – commanded to disappear supernaturally or to move out of the body harmlessly. BELIEVE FOR THE IMPOSSIBLE TO COME TO PASS AND THAT IS EXACTLY WHAT HAPPENS.

A non-malignant tumor has no spirit life and it will disappear when you command it to "wither away" and vanish.

ALL SICKNESS AND DISEASE IS NOT A SPIRIT. JESUS DISTINGUISHED BETWEEN EVIL SPIRITS ON THE ONE HAND AND SICKNESS AND DISEASE ON THE OTHER (Matthew 10:1; Acts 19:11-12). Sickness and disease can, however, be INFLICTED by the power of Satan (Job 2:7). Even though the sickens or disease is not caused by a spirit, the remedy is the same – the same as for burns and injuries. You command it to go in the Name of Jesus and immediately the God-implanted ability of the human body to heal itself swings into action because the hindrance has been removed.

Demons have the power to DUPLICATE THE SAME OLD SYMPTOMS in those who have been healed. Here we have Satan's favorite weapon in action, THE POWER OF THE LIE – induced pains and 'feelings' to make the victim doubt that God has ever done anything permanent for him. Here is a man in double bondage, and there is very real danger that if he continues to BELIEVE AND CONFESS THE DEVIL'S LIE he will have the old trouble back in reality. The lying spirit is revealed, bound and ordered to depart. Then THE SYMPTOMS CEASE.

At this point Tom made a comment to those who may not feel they have adequate gifts. ARE YOU GETTING RESULTS! What more could be desired? The main thing is that THE JOB IS GETTING DONE. We don't need to know all about the person we pray for, but we do need to get him or her delivered. There are differences in ministries and the same gift operates differently in different people (1 Corinthians 12:5-6). Use the gifts God has given you. Don't despise others who have more gifts. All gifts are needed to properly do the work to which God has called them.

# HEALING THROUGH REPENTANCE AND FORGIVENESS

A major block to healing is unforgiveness. Take a look at Mark 11:25 where it explains the principle of giving and receiving forgiveness.

> **²⁵ And when you stand praying, if you hold anything against anyone, forgive them, so that your father in heaven may forgive you your sins,"**
> Mark 11: 25

Note that there is this general statement about prayer: "AND WHENEVER YOU STAND PRAYING". This is talking about every time we approach God in prayer that we should be aware of our condition of forgiveness. Next it explains that, "if you have anything against anyone, forgive him". Again a very clear statement. We as Christians are not allowed to hold on to unforgiveness. The condition of forgiveness allows this line to apply: "that your Father in heaven may also forgive you your trespasses". If we hold on to unforgiveness then God, our Father in heaven, withholds forgiveness for our trespasses. To receive God's forgiveness we must forgive others, including forgiving God and ourselves.

When we are trying to pray to God while hold unforgiveness, our prayers become less effective and in fact there is a danger that He might not answer any of our prayers because we are operating in sin.

Therefore it is important for us to repent for our sin, to forgive and then pray for specific intentions.

## PRACTICAL STEPS TO FORGIVENESS:

1) Make a decision to forgive.
   – Forgiveness is not a feeling.
2) Repent and release the hurt.
   – Hurt can be described as hatred, bitterness and resentment
   – These are doors to evil spirits.
   – Close the doors to evil.
3) Forgive God, yourself and others!
4) Ask God's blessing on the other person and yourself and the situation.

## HEALING BY THE WORD OF COMMAND

Let's read Mark 11: 22-24:

> **[22] "Have faith in God," Jesus answered. [23] "Truly I tell you, if anyone says to this mountain, 'Go, throw yourself into the sea,' and does not doubt in their heart but believes that what they say will happen, it will be done for them. [24] Therefore I tell you, whatever you ask for in prayer, believe that you have received it, and it will be yours.**

According to Mark 11:22-24 it is in order to PRAY for things to happen, and it is also in order to COMMAND, things to happen. The latter method, frequently mentioned in the Scriptures, is the one usually used in ministering a gift of healing. For further information on this subject, refer to Chapter nine, the Gift of Miracles.

## ATTENTION READER

In conclusion, may I, Tom, state most emphatically that I have no quarrel whatsoever with the medical profession whose praiseworthy efforts and noble achievements have been a great blessing to the human race. The doctor knows that the human body has the ability to heal itself, and by his skill he endeavors to remove whatever is causing the trouble in order that nature may take over and healing may result. This is a good thing for, as the Apostle Paul has said, "all men have not faith" (2 Thessalonians 3:2 KJV) and multitudes of earth's millions would be in a sorry plight if it were not for modern medicine.

What I am presenting here is something for the CHRISTIAN, the SPIRIT-FILLED CHRISTIAN – a more excellent way of going directly to God to receive help in time of need. This way the results are quicker and also perfect,

> **"Every good gift and every perfect gift is from above, and cometh down from the Father of lights, with whom is no variableness, neither shadow of turning."**
> James 1: 17 KJV

Moreover, this is for medically HOPELESS cases; FOR WHERE MAN'S BEST EFFORTS MUST FAIL, IS THE PLACE WHERE THE POWER OF GOD MOVES IN AND TAKES OVER.

# CHAPTER NINE
# THE GIFT OF MIRACLES
# 1 Corinthians 12:10

THE GIFT OF MIRACLES IS THE GOD GIVEN ABILITY TO PERFORM MIRACLES.

Miracles belong to the realm of the supernatural, the sphere in which God has made us laborer's with Him. Let us not fall into the mistake of many theologians who attempt to explain miracles. They are nowhere explained by God and consequently cannot be explained by man. Nevertheless, though the Bible does not EXPLAIN a single miracle, it does outline four successive steps which when taken by a Spirit-filled believer will RESULT in a miracle.

## FOUR STEPS TO A MIRACLE

Here are the four steps:

1. HEARING the word of the Lord. (Thus you are given God's blueprint for the job and His green-light, go-ahead signal for action on your part).

2. BELIEVING the word of the Lord when you hear it. (The faith for a miracle always comes by hearing God's word).

3. SPEAKING the word of the Lord that it may come to pass. (Commanding it done in the Name of Jesus).

4. BELIEVING the word of the Lord AS YOU SPEAK IT. (Believing that it will SURELY come to pass).


In each of these four steps we find THE WORD OF THE LORD mentioned. Have we any Scriptural authority for this? Yes. Read carefully 1 Kings 13:1-5 KJV, noting especially the emphasis upon "THE WORD OF THE LORD".

The prophet came "BY THE WORD OF THE LORD". He cried against the altar "IN THE WORD OF THE LORD".

He said, "O altar, THUS SAITH THE LORD – Behold the altar shall be rent."

"And it came to pass . . . that the altar was rent . . . according to the sign which the man of God had given BY THE WORD OF THE LORD".

The word of the Lord SPOKEN BY MAN split the altar.


Now turn to Ezekiel 37:1-10, (the story of the Valley of Dry Bones), a chapter which contains the ingredients of a miracle.

Ezekiel heard the word of the Lord – "Prophesy – say unto them – bones, hear the word of the Lord."

He used God's WORDS, the same words. ("So I prophesied AS I WAS COMMANDED").

The word of God produced results when spoken. ("As I prophesied, behold a shaking.")

Moses likewise heard the word of the Lord before he performed his numerous miracles. So also did Joshua. He first spoke to the Lord before he commanded the sun to stand still. (Joshua 10:12)

Elijah said, "I have done all these things AT THY WORD". (1 Kings 18:36-38 KJV) Peter prayed to know God's will before he commanded Dorcas to rise from the dead. (Acts 9:40)

Now let us go back and one by one discuss in detail the four steps to a miracle.

# FOUR STEPS TO A MIRACLE EXPLAINED

**1. HEARING THE WORD OF THE LORD.** Faith comes by hearing God's voice and knowing His will. (Romans 10:17). Without hearing there can be no believing; and without believing there can be no action on our part; and if we do not ACT there can be no MIRACLE. Abraham heard God's voice and it conveyed such ASSURANCE to Abraham that he obeyed, and "WENT OUT NOT KNOWING WHITHER HE WENT" (Hebrews 11: 8 KJV). Moses in Exodus heard from God and it generated such FAITH in his heart that a man of eighty went back single-handed to contend with and triumph over the king and his kingdom.

The word of the Lord is just as sure to YOU when you hear it giving YOU the fortitude to act on it with equal confidence for a miracle.

This, my brother/sister, is the reason why you and I MUST HAVE REVELATION GIFTS IN OPERATION in order that we in our day may HEAR, and KNOW, and BELIEVE, and ACT, and see MIRACLES to the glory of God.

## 2. BELIEVING THE WORD OF THE LORD WHEN YOU HEAR IT.

To hear the word of the Lord with such FORCE, CLARITY AND ASSURANCE that you CAN BELIEVE FOR AN OUTSTANDING MIRACLE your revelation gifts MUST BE OPERATING in their fullness. This in turn necessitates a life of prayer, tongues, revelation, the Word, a close walk with God, self-denial, and a continuous consciousness of His presence whether waking or sleeping. Less than this will suffice for lesser miracles – and you will have them because of God-given abilities within – but how much more glorious to have these abilities operating in their fullness as they will when you are "filled with ALL THE FULNESS OF GOD". (Ephesians 3:19 KJV)

Do not misunderstand me here. By observing a close walk with God YOU DO NOT MERIT ANYTHING – no, not the value of a pin. YOU ARE MERELY putting yourself in a place where THE GRACE OF GOD which is wholly apart from your own good works CAN WORK IN YOU to an extent never before realized. (Read Galatians 3:5). Let me shout this in your ears: From salvation to glory, from beginning to end it's all grace, GRACE, G-R-A-C-E-! The men in our generation, who will do the "greater works", will be grace men. (John 14:12)

## 3. SPEAKING THE WORD OF THE LORD THAT IT MAY COME TO PASS.

God uses his own IRRESISTIBLE WORDS to bring things to pass. In creation it was the word of God that spoke the world into existence.

> **"By the word of the Lord were the heavens made FOR HE SPAKE and it was done".**
> Psalms 33:6-9 KJV

Moses and the prophets spoke GOD'S IRRESISTIBLE WORDS and miracles were the result.

When Jesus came, He used words – THE IRRESISTIBLE WORDS OF HIS FATHER. He did not use His own words. There was a reason for this. God's words are SPIRIT and LIFE (John 6:63). They are also POWER (Luke 4:32, 36). Even the Roman centurion knew this, He said to Jesus,

> **"SPEAK THE WORD only and my servant shall be healed".**
> Matthew 8:8 KJV

In numerous instances in which Jesus healed the sick and wrought miracles, He invariably spoke it, commanded it or declared it done.

Believers likewise use GOD'S IRRESISTIBLE WORDS. Jesus said "I have given unto THEM the WORDS which Thou gavest Me." (John 17:8,14 KJV) We have been given the same authority to speak God's words as Jesus had. We are not speaking of PRAYING but of SAYING. Jesus said to his disciples,

> **"Thou shalt SAY to this mountain . . .".**
> Mark 11:23 KJV

True, we must pray. (Mark 11:24)

> **"Men ought ALWAYS to pray."**
> Luke 18:1 KJV

In fact, it is only through MUCH PRAYER AND COMMUNION WITH GOD that we are able to SPEAK HIS WORDS EFFECTIVELY. Thus it is that we know the mind and the will of the Father and the words He would have us speak. Jesus who sometimes spent whole nights in prayer said,

> **"I do nothing of Myself but as my Father hath taught Me I SPEAK."**
> John 8: 28 KJV (See also John 12:49, 50)

The creative word which Jesus spoke before the eyes of men was EXACTLY what He had been SHOWN (Note the word "SEETH") and TOLD by His Father (John 5:19 KJV).

Regarding our authority as believers, hear the words of Jesus:

> **"As Thou hast sent Me into the world EVEN SO have I sent THEM into the world."**
> John 17:18 KJV

Just as the Father authorized the Son, so the Son has given us the same authority, the same power, the same irresistible words to speak. He said,

> **"In my Name shall they (YE) cast out devils".**
> Mark 16:17 KJV

> "Ye shall say to this mountain, Remove . . . **AND NOTHING SHALL BE IMPOSSIBLE TO YOU**"
> Matthews 17:20 KJV

# THE TWO FOLD POWER OF THE WORD OF GOD

A. The WORD OF GOD is CREATIVE – calling into existence.
B. The WORD OF GOD is DESTRUCTIVE – commanding existence to cease.

Just as the word of God spoke the world into being so the same word when spoken by you has CREATIVE POWER to call into existence things which are not – health, strength, life, new parts and organs in the human body; and in the spiritual realm, things spiritual. Romans 4:17 KJV says that: "God calls the things which be not, as though, they were." Even so, you speak THE WORD to nonexistent things just as though they exist, and they obey and come into being. God says,

> **"I am the Lord that confirmeth the words of my servants".**
> Isaiah 44:26 KJV

> **"I hasten (stand by) my word to perform it."**
> Jeremiah 1:12 KJV

But not only is God's word in your mouth creative. It is also a word to CAST DOWN, to BRING TO NAUGHT and TO DESTROY.

> **"Is not my word AS A FIRE, saith the Lord, and AS A HAMMER that BREAKS the rocks in pieces. He that hath my word LET HIM SPEAK MY WORD faithfully."**
> Jeremiah 23:28,29 KJV

The words which Jesus spoke to the fig tree destroyed it at the very root.

You may ask the question, "How can I speak such a word?" Just listen to the words in the following sentences, spoken in the faith of God they worked miracles:

> "I command you, bone growth – CEASE TO exist."
> "Poisons, PASS HARMLESSLY from this body."
> "Brain pattern, BE BROKEN UP completely that you may no longer be a hindrance to right thinking."
> "GERMS, DIE."
> "Piece of steel embedded in this eyeball, DISAPPEAR MIRACULOUSLY." (It did, although for twelve years it had lodged there causing intense discomfort.)
> "In the Name of Jesus we command the work of the Enemy in this body to DISAPPEAR COMPLETELY that there may be restoration and recovery."

Sometimes the spoken word commands that which should not be present to disappear; and then commands that which should be to come into existence.

Sometimes there are two creative acts. Tom's sister and her husband were eye-witnesses of a miracle where by a blind man received sight. The brother who was ministering first commanded in the Name of Jesus that eyeballs come up in the empty sockets. They appeared immediately but there was no sight in them. (Compare Ezekiel 37:8) He then commanded the eyes to receive sight; and the man saw. The following night he was back again in the meeting rejoicing in what God had done for him.

The EASIEST way, the BEST way, to speak GOD'S IRRESISTIBLE WORDS is to be FULL of the Holy Ghost when you speak. In Acts the pattern seems to be: "He, FILLED with the Holy Ghost, SAID." Filled with the Spirit, you speak as one who prophesies, and I need not remind you that he who prophesies speaks as he is MOVED by THE HOLY GHOST. You do not use your own words; you are speaking God's words as the Spirit gives you the words to utter; and it is God's words which have POWER. This is the ideal way to minister miracles. I, Tom believe, that this is THE WAY IN WHICH MOST, IF NOT ALL, OUTSTANDING MIRACLES ARE WROUGHT.

NEVERTHELESS – and I, Tom, want to EMPHASIZE this – there have been times when I was very, very tired, the assurance of the Spirit was faint, and I didn't FEEL very much of anything. I KNEW, however, that I had the gifts which God had given, and I HAD CONFIDENCE in THE POWER OF THE NAME OF JESUS so I commanded in the name of Jesus – and the miracle took place.

**4.** And now, the fourth step to a miracle:

**BELIEVING THE WORD OF THE LORD AS YOU SPEAK IT.**

Jesus, when speaking of miracles, said,

> **"Whosoever shall say to this mountain, Be thou cast into the sea; AND SHALL NOT DOUBT IN HIS HEART but shall believe that those things which he saith shall come to pass; he shall have whatsoever he saith."**
> Mark 11:23 KJV

# HOW DO YOU KEEP FROM DOUBTING IN YOUR HEART?

Here is the answer:

When commenting on step three I stated that:

a) TO BE FULL OF THE HOLY SPIRIT ENSURES that you speak God's words. But it ensures more than that.

b) TO BE FULL OF THE HOLY SPIRIT ENSURES THAT you speak God's words WITHOUT DOUBT IN YOUR HEART.

You are SO FULL of God's blessed Holy Spirit that doubt can find no room in your heart. The Spirit fills and controls your entire being with AN OVERWHELMING AND UNSHAKEABLE ASSURANCE that THIS is the will of God, and that the time is NOW.

Paul said:

> **"Christ liveth in me".**
> Galatians 2:20 KJV
>
> **"Christ speaketh in me".**
> Galatians 4:6; 2 Corinthians 13:3 KJV

It was CHRIST SPEAKING when the fig tree was cursed. THEREFORE the miracle had to take place.

It was the Spirit of CHRIST SPEAKING in the prophets (1 Peter 1:11). THEREFORE when they spoke the miracles had to happen.

It is CHRIST SPEAKING in YOU when, filled with the Spirit, you declare and command. THEREFORE believe it, do not doubt it, and the miracle – YOUR *(CHRIST'S)* MIRACLE – will come to pass.

Some years ago just before a service in a place where I, Tom, was a complete stranger, God told me that I was to minister 'an outstanding miracle' to a certain child who would be brought to the church. Later, in the service, I pointed out the child to the people and prayed for him. Within three days the top of his head, which had always been greatly enlarged. had come to normal size and the Lord had touched his mind also. It was a matter of ministering before the eyes of men what God had previously revealed in the place of prayer. This is in harmony with what we read in John 5:19:

> **" Jesus gave them this answer: "Very truly I tell you, the Son can do nothing by himself; he can do only what he sees his Father doing, because whatever the Father does the Son also does."**

It is interesting to note that whenever the word of the Lord comes in this manner – a sudden, unasked-for revelation of God's will – and you act on the revelation in faith and obedience, a miracle will invariably result.

On the other hand, when man in his need requests prayer and you minister to him, it can sometimes happen that the results will be little or nothing even though God shows you that it IS HIS will to heal and deliver.

More than once a man of God has prayed for an afflicted one, has declared God's deliverance to him – and the man has got worse and died.

WHAT IS THE ANSWER? Years ago I, Tom, asked the Lord about this and He immediately directed me to 2 Kings 13:14-19. Here we find the two sides, God's side and man's side. God's declared will in the matter was FULL DELIVERANCE, exactly one hundred percent. "THE LORD'S DELIVERANCE" IS ALWAYS COMPLETE DELIVERANCE – "Thou shalt smite the Syrians TILL THOU HAVE CONSUMED THEM".

But in this case God was not acting alone. Man had cried out in his weakness and extremity and therefore God would permit the final outcome TO BE DEPENDENT ON THE FAITH AND OBEDIENCE OF MAN. MAN MUST ACT – "Smite upon the ground". (This is from the story of Elisha and the King of Israel in 2 Kings 13:16-20). Six in the Bible is the number of man. To bring to pass God's perfect deliverance God requires no more than man is capable of doing. Had the king struck six times God would have granted perfect deliverance, but man limited God to only three victories. MAN MUST ACT IN FAITH.

Learn from this that not merely must you ACT IN FAITH TO THE LIMIT OF GOD'S REVEALED WILL, you must also when necessary RAISE THE FAITH of the man in need. By ministering the Word, Paul first raised the faith of a crippled man. Then Paul looked upon the spirit of the man "and perceiving that HE HAD FAITH TO BE THEN HEALED, he commanded a miracle." (Acts 14:8-10 KJV)

When ministering to the sick NEVER, NEVER tell people that they have no faith. They have come for help and not to be lectured and beaten down. MINISTER ENCOURAGEMENT. Give them the WORD. Build them up spiritually and their faith will come up to the level of your gift.

# EXPECT A MIRACLE

Even if a man has no faith whatever, EXPECT A MIRACLE if God gives you the green light to go ahead. One night I, Tom, sat at a kitchen table visiting a Christian couple. The man suffering from a serious heart condition said with tears, "I have no faith left". "And I", said his wife, "have no faith whatever". Suddenly, moved mightily by the Spirit of God, I brought my fist smashing down in the center of the table and I shouted, "I don't care if you have no faith! I am full of faith - the faith of God!" Then I said to the man, "Won't you please let me pray for you anyway? I want to." He nodded agreement, and as I laid my hands on him the healing power of God struck him and surged through his body to such an extent that he could hardly say a word for ten minutes.

But what if you are in the dark concerning God's will? Have you any right to expect a miracle?

In 1 Kings 17:17-24, the Bible records AN OUTSTANDING MIRACLE which is AN EXCEPTION TO THE FOUR STEP GENERAL RULE, which we have been studying. Here there is no word of the Lord to give faith and direction, no miracle-producing word of the Lord for His servant to speak. Let us see what Elijah does in such a situation.

1. Taking the dead child from the arms of its mother and swiftly ascending to this room above, He

TAKES THE ENTIRE SITUATION OUT OF THE REALM OF HUMAN HOPELESSNESS AND HE CARRIES IT INTO THE VERY REALM OF THE SUPERNATURAL where he dwells in the presence of God and where God always meets with HIM.

2. He puts the boy IN HIS OWN BED. Now it is his own need and his own burden which the prophet lays before God.

3. He places his confidence in the mercy of God.

4. He cries out to God in FERVENT PRAYER and he receives an answer.

Let us learn from this incident that THE GIFT OF FAITH in a believer can stand alone, and cry out, and claim a miracle and receive from God.

Jesus mentioned both kinds of miracles; the one in which you command the miracle and the one in which you pray. (Mark 11:22-24)

> **"When ye pray, believe that ye RECEIVE them and ye SHALL HAVE them."**
> Mark 11: 24 KJV

And now a word to God's ministering servant. You have taken your place in humility before God. Now take your place in boldness and confidence before men.

Elisha said, "Let him come unto Me and he shall know that there is a prophet in Israel." (2 Kings 5: 8 KJV)

Peter said, "Such as I HAVE give I unto thee." (Acts 3: 6 KJV)

Strong language, but not the tongue of human pride and boasting. THESE MEN KNEW whose they were and what they had received. SO DO YOU!

Men cannot see and hear God but they see you and they hear you speak God's words. BE BOLD. Jesus said,

> **"He that heareth you heareth Me."**
> Luke 10: 16 KJV

If God gives you a personal word of knowledge concerning the person with whom you are dealing, DECLARE IT as Jesus did (John 4:17, 18) that man may know that this is of God and may believe.

The child mentioned in John 4:50 was healed BECAUSE "THE MAN BELIEVED THE WORD WHICH JESUS HAD SPOKEN to him." When you minister, TELL MEN THAT THEY MUST BELIEVE AND ACT IN FAITH UPON YOUR WORDS.

As I, Tom, prayed for a lady with cancer, God showed me that she was healed. A week later she was still suffering intensely and was greatly discouraged. I said, "No, I can't pray again that God will heal you because I AM SHOWN that cancer as completely gone. YOU MUST BELIEVE WHAT I TELL YOU." Once a week for a whole month I had to insist that she was healed. Each time I stood fast on God's revelation, and said, "You must believe what I say. God says, **'I am the Lord that confirmeth the words of MY servants.'** (Isaiah 44:26 KJV) Believe, what I tell you." Then suddenly every pain and symptom vanished and in thirteen years there has been no recurrence.

Listen to John 14:12 KJV:

> **"VERILY, VERILY I SAY UNTO YOU, HE THAT BELIEVETH ON ME THE WORKS THAT I DO SHALL HE DO ALSO; AND GREATER WORKS THAN THESE SHALL YE DO."**

This is Jesus' word to you.

Too long the church of God has feared to go too far and hesitated to expect too much. Let us realize that surely Jesus said what He meant and He meant what He said . . . Otherwise this verse is valueless!

Jesus attached ONLY ONE CONDITION to this promise – THAT YOU BELIEVE WHAT HE SAID. Hear His words again:

> **"MOST ASSUREDLY AND MOST EMPHATICALLY I SAY TO YOU, HE WHO STEADFASTLY BELIEVES IN ME WILL HIMSELF BE ABLE TO DO THE THINGS THAT I DO, AND HE WILL EVEN DO GREATER THINGS THAN THESE."**
> John 14: 12 (Version unknown)

The mind cannot grasp this and even the spiritual comprehension of redeemed men CANNOT take it in and contain the fullness of it. GOD MUST REVEAL IT TO YOU BY HIS SPIRIT "that you may KNOW the THINGS THAT ARE FREELY GIVEN TO YOU BY GOD" (1 Corinthians 2: 12) . You, my brother, must MEDITATE MUCH on this verse and WAIT ON GOD that He may ABUNDANTLY REVEAL to you the height and breadth and length and depth of this marvelous promise which is to you. THEN you will always find it easier to believe than to doubt, easier to act than to hesitate, easier to move at the miracle level than below it.

# CHAPTER TEN
# THE MIRACLE OF
# RAISING THE DEAD

We find it recorded that both Elijah and Elisha raised the dead (1 Kings 17:17; 2 Kings 4:32; 13:21). Jesus also raised the dead (Luke 7:11-17, Luke 8:40-56, John 11:17-44). In Matthew 10:8 He commanded His disciples to do likewise:

> **"Heal the sick . . . RAISE THE DEAD, Cast out devils."**

John 11 verse 17-20 makes it plain that the instructions contained in this chapter were to continue in force at a later date when the Gospel would be proclaimed by the church throughout the whole Gentile world. In harmony with this thought, we read that Peter and Paul were both used by God to raise the dead. (Acts 9:40 and 20:10).

It is to be noted that though Jesus healed all who came to Him, He did not make a general practice of raising the dead. Neither did the disciples, though a few instances are recorded. Just as in our own day there have been a few well-authenticated cases. We may therefore infer that this miracle was not to be of frequent occurrence – certainly not at that time. Nevertheless, the fact that Jesus DID command it and that the early church carried out this commandment leaves us no alternative than to conclude that RAISING THE DEAD IS STILL IN ORDER FOR THE CHURCH OF TODAY. It may well be that in the closing days of this dispensation of grace, all kinds of signs, miracles and wonders will again abound and the church, clothed with great power and authority, will witness throughout the world to THE RESURRECTION OF JESUS CHRIST, the coming King of Glory. This has been the opinion of many sane, sound, outstanding Christian leaders among whom were A. B. Simpson, founder of the Christian and Missionary Alliance, Smith Wigglesworth and the late Dr. Price [5].

In recent years there has been an ever increasing buildup of Satanic power and wickedness on every hand, and it would seem that countless multitudes of demons are taking over more and more in the world of men. God, however, has not forsaken His people, and to some of his outstanding servants He has given revelation concerning A BRIEF PERIOD OF POWER AND VICTORY FOR HIS CHURCH SUCH AS IT HAS NEVER PREVIOUSLY EXPERIENCED. That outstanding miracles and "greater works" will play a leading part in God's program is certain. Already, in confirmation of this fact, the TIDE OF FAITH IS RISING.

(Note: What I, Tom, have just stated is NOT to be regarded as advocating or endorsing in any way the Man-child teaching with its "manifested sons" and its devious, unscriptural byways which as in the past invariably end in heresy and confusion. The Central theme to Manifest Sons of God doctrine is the belief that the Christian life, has levels to go through, to reach maturity. The first level is that of servant of God, the next is that of friend of God, following this is to become a son of God and the realization of gods ourselves.)

"But why," some will ask, "are you laying particular stress upon this miracle of raising the dead?"

1. Because it is commanded in the Word.

2. Because sometime you will stand beside one who is dying and YOU will need to rebuke the power of death. Now is the time to prepare yourself.

3. Because it COULD happen that a day will come when acting in the center of God's revealed will, YOU will command a miracle in the Name of Jesus and by the gift of Discerning of Spirits will actually see the human spirit moving back again into the body which it had left. I, Tom, am speaking now in personal testimony and from personal experience. Such a miracle as this is possible because you previously prepared yourself for just such an emergency. Learn a lesson from the commando. In the moment of danger and violence he does instantly and almost instinctively what previous months of combat training have ALREADY TRAINED mind and muscle to do.

4. Finally, the fact that you have set your sights on raising the dead and on greater works than Jesus did WILL ABSOLUTELY ENSURE that your faith for other miracles and for healings will be VERY, VERY HIGH INDEED. He who aims at a star will not shoot low.

In closing, it should not be necessary to emphasize the following facts: Raising the dead HAS TO BE IN GOD'S WILL. Furthermore, YOU have to KNOW that it is in God's will, because God does not uphold what He has not authorized. This is why PETER PRAYED before raising Dorcas. (Acts 9: 36-42) Some in self-will have intruded into this field bringing humiliation upon themselves by their presumption, and also bringing reproach and ridicule upon the work of God in general. God is not glorified in fanaticism.

# CHAPTER ELEVEN CASTING OUT DEVILS

Jesus speaking of the casting out of a devil, called it a MIRACLE, or "WORK OF POWER" (Mark 9:38, 39). Therefore to cast out a demon brings the Gift of Miracles into operation. THE POWER, THE GOD-GIVEN ABILITY TO PERFORM THE ACT, IS IN YOU.

The casting out of devils is part of the great commission to those who preach the Gospel.

> **"In my name shall they cast out devils."**
> Mark 16:17 KJV

In this connection read Luke 10:17-20 KJV, carefully noting especially the following verses.

Verse 17: **"The devils are SUBJECT UNTO US through Thy Name."** Meditate upon this. Act upon it. Boldly declare it: "Devil, you are subject to me in this matter". The source of your power and authority is altogether and solely in THE NAME OF JESUS and all that the Name of Jesus stands for. So USE THE NAME as the early church used it. Use it in prayer and use it to command miracles. (If possible, get E.W. Kenyon's book, *The Wonderful Name of Jesus* and read it.[6] You should have ALL of Kenyon's works!)

Verse 18: "I give unto YOU POWER OVER ALL THE POWER OF THE ENEMY." At all times, in all places, upon every field of conflict, you have power overall the power of the enemy.

Verse 19: **"And nothing shall by any means harm you."** This is true. The insane, the violently drunk, the knife held at your throat are not to be feared. The demons already fear the power which is in you, knowing that you can bind them and cast them out. (James 2:19)

Do not ASK demons to leave. They do not appreciate or respond to politeness. The devil will obey nothing but AN ABSOLUTE COMMAND.

Do not waste time encouraging demons to give you information. All demons are liars (John 8:44) and deceivers (In Genesis 3:1-5 Eve is deceived.) "Jesus suffered not the spirits to speak." (Mark 1: 34, Luke 4:41) Through the gift of the Word of Knowledge and the gift of Discerning of Spirits, you have direct access to all the information you may require, so command them to be silent, and concentrate on casting them out.

DO NOT PRAY TO GOD and beg Him to resist the devil and cast him out. The Bible says that "GOD resisteth the proud," (James 4: 6 KJV) but to YOU He says, "Resist the devil and he will flee from you" (James 4: 7). DO NOT ask Jesus to come down and cast him out and heal. Jesus gave YOU the power TO COMMAND IT. THE DEVIL HEEDS THE AUTHORITY GIVEN YOU BY THE HOLY GHOST.

DO NOT "Plead the Blood" (whatever that means) over a case of demon affliction. Claim the power and authority of the Blood, enforce the victory of the Blood, believe and know that you are ALREADY a conqueror because of what THE BLOOD OF JESUS has forever accomplished on your behalf. Now, ON THE BASIS OF THIS, speak God's word and overcome by the Blood (Read Revelations 12:11 below). Declare it: "Devil, it is written, we overcome you by the Blood!"

> **[11] And they overcame him by the blood of the Lamb, and by the word of their testimony; and they loved not their lives unto the death.**
> Revelation 12:11

DO NOT tell people in the congregation to bow their heads and be reverent and pray lest a demon which has been cast out should enter one of them. YOU command the binding of a powerful, violent spirit before you cast him out and you will find that he will not trouble anyone.

In general it is best to deal with such spirits when only a few established believers full of faith are present. In any multitude there are always the fearful and unbelieving present and this can to a certain extent be a hindrance.

Is it necessary to fast before casting out demons? No, not if you are FULL of the Holy Ghost. If you are under par spiritually, you SHOULD fast or do anything else that will get you into proper condition – even if you don't have a bout with the devil coming up.

# EDITOR'S NOTE: THE AUTHOR'S LIST OF EXPECTATIONS OF A BELIEVER

In Chapter Two under 'IMPORTANT – TO MAINTAIN THE OPERATION OF THIS GIFT AND ALL THE GIFTS', the author has outline expectations of a believer who is full of the Holy Spirit.

These are: let your words be few, that one must be in relationship with God: Father, His Son Jesus and His Holy Spirit, commit to pray, be continually strengthened by scripture, be active in their faith, be humble, speaking much in other tongues and finally that you know your position in the Holy Spirit - *live in the Spirit, walk in the Spirit*.

To understand your position with the Holy Spirit you might refer again to 'WHEN OPERATING SPIRITUAL GIFTS', found in the Introduction.

# PROCEDURE WHEN CASTING OUT DEVILS.

**1.** By the gift of Discerning of Spirits FIND OUT WHICH SPIRIT or spirits are present, and ALSO THE NAME or names. It is a well-known fact that in many cases, especially when the person is possessed by powerful controlling spirits, the demons will not leave unless called by name (Mark 5: 1-15). Sometimes, instead of a name, you will by the gift of Discerning of Spirits be shown something in a vision, which will enable you to identify the spirit. It may be something resembling a human form; or some kind of weapon (gun, dagger, arrow); or some sort of living creature (serpent, octopus, bird of prey, etc.). Symbols were similarly used throughout the book of Revelation. (Note Revelations 16:13-14) The main characteristics of whatever you are shown will indicate the distinctive character of the demon spirit who is causing the trouble.

**2.** You BIND the intruder in the Name of Jesus. (Mark 3:26-27; Matthew 18:18)

**3.** Calling him by name, you command him to leave. In many cases it is advisable to use the word "power" instead of "demon" or "spirit". You thus avoid raising doubts and questions in the minds of the uninformed. For example: "Power of drug addiction, I command . . . ". Also when you are dealing with something revealed by vision, it is better not to mention WHAT you have been shown. Just say, "In the Name of Jesus, I command THAT WHICH IS REVEALED to be bound and to come out."

**4.** Having commanded the demon to leave, let the Spirit of God witness to you that the intruder has really gone. This is important. It is also necessary to make sure that no other spirits are still present to cause further trouble.

If the demon will not obey and persistently refuses to leave, you have absolute right and authority to command him to descend into the pit, (also rendered "bottomless pit" and "deep"). The Lord instructed me to take this course of action one night many years ago when in the presence of a crowd of people, a stubborn demon had us utterly defeated. From what is recorded in the Word, it would seem that Jesus merely cast the demons out of people (See Matthew 8:16, 28-34). That He could also send them down to the pit (Luke 8:31) and that they would be tormented there before the final day of judgment (Matthew 8:29) were frightening possibilities of which the demons seemed well aware.

**5.** Should it happen – this is a matter of rare occurrence – that a demon will not heed the command to go into the pit, you have reason to suspect – and revelation gifts will confirm it – that this lesser power is being upheld by one of Satan's higher powers or by Satan, himself. In such a case, BIND THE HIGHER POWERS. "Satan and you higher powers, I command you to be bound in the Name of Jesus, that you cannot uphold this lesser power."

6. Now, once again, command the disobedient spirit to go into the pit. Usually there is immediate response.

If, however, there is continued refusal for a time, just continue to command and insist UNTIL HE LEAVES, whether it takes minutes or hours. Rest assured that you have now taken EVERY step to ensure victory, so keep on until you win. It is surprising how your faith and determination will continue to rise as you do so! You have all the time in the world to finish the job. Having started, NEVER, NEVER, NEVER GIVE UP. A few years ago at the Bow Valley Camp Meeting, we battled for several hours for the deliverance of a man of twenty-five who all his life had been deaf and dumb There were many spirits present, but finally the last spirit moved out and the man heard. The first word we taught him to say was "Jesus".

## CONCLUSION:

In conclusion, let me say that there will be some who will wonder if I, Tom, have been a little extreme in advocating such literal interpretation of the Word and such out-and-out action upon what it declares. They may also question some of the methods I have suggested in these pages.

It is true that some of what I have written is new and different; but must it therefore be Scripturally unsound and must my methods as a result be impractical and unsuccessful? Did you ever reflect on the fact that the Bible is full of things new and different and surprising? A floating axe-head, a bush burning yet not consumed, mud applied to the eyes of the blind to enable him to see, the bones of a dead prophet imparting life to a corpse.

The methods which I, Tom, have outlined in this course are methods which I myself have used and put to the test countless times over the past eighteen years. In homes, in local services, at camp meeting seminars, I have taught and demonstrated publicly what I have here laid down, and God has graciously blessed my efforts. To Him be all the glory.

The incident which I have just related concerning the deaf and dumb man is only one of a great number of cases in which THE RESULTS HAVE PROVEN THE SOUNDNESS OF THE METHODS USED.

You remember the story of Naaman, the Syrian, (2 Kings 5), and how the prophet of God told him to dip seven times in the Jordan that he might be miraculously healed. Naaman did not receive anything until he humbled himself and followed a method that he did not like.

BUT IT PRODUCES RESULTS – and Naaman was overjoyed at what he received.

*SO WILL YOU, MY FRIEND, BE OVERJOYED*
*AS IN FAITH AND KNOWLEDGE*
*YOU MOVE OUT*
*INTO THE GLORIOUS MINISTRY*
*OF SPIRITUAL GIFTS.*

*Tom Roycroft*

# NOTES:

[1] Tommy Lee Osborn was born on December 23, 1923 died February 14, 2013. More information can be found on Osborn Ministries International website: https://osborn.org .

[2] Sherrill, John L., They Speak With Other Tongues, Chosen Books, 1999. (It was originally published 1964). In 1970, John Sherrill founded a publishing company - Chosen Books.

[3] Ellicott D.D., Charles John, The Commentary For Schools (New Testament), Cassell, Petter, Galpin & Co., London, Paris and New York, 1879.

[4] This book is not meant to be a forum for discussion of homosexuality, but rather to explain how to minister spiritual gifts.

I, Kenneth, have found that healing has occurred in individuals who have chosen to overcoming unwanted same-sexual attractions.

I take the position that biological, psychological and social factors shape sexual identity at an early age for most people. Further that there is no such thing as a 'gay gene' and there is no evidence to support the idea that homosexuality is simply genetic. This position then opens the field to healing and wholeness through Jesus Christ.

I refer you to http://www.narth.com the website for the National Association for Research and Therapy of Homosexuality, NARTH. This site is now being redirected to www.therapeuticchoice.com .

On that site you can find many scientific and professional studies examining homosexuality:

- *NARTH's Response to the American Psychological Association's Claims on Homosexuality.* – This paper examines over 100 years of scientific literature on the subject of overcoming unwanted sexual attractions.

- *Identical Twin Studies Demonstrate Homosexuality is Not Genetic* by Dr. Neil Whitehead.

- *Practice Guidelines for the Treatment of Unwanted Same Sex Attractions and Behavior* – These guidelines are intended for the treatment of clients who experience unwanted same-sex attractions (SSA) and behavior.

- *Right to Treatment* – The NARTH Alliance respects each client's dignity, autonomy and free agency. We believe that clients have the right to claim a gay identity, or to diminish their homosexuality and to develop their heterosexual potential.

[5] A. B. Simpson (Albert Benjamin Simpson 1843-1919), founder of the Christian and Missionary Alliance, Smith Wigglesworth (1859-1947), and Dr. Price (Charles Sydney Price 1887-1947).

[6] Essek William Kenyon 1867- 1948. His book is available in PDF on the internet, on YouTube and in both paperback and eBook – reference: Kenyon, E.W., The Wonderful Name of Jesus. Contact: Kenyon's Gospel Publishing Society, PO Box 973, Lynnwood, WA 98046-0973 - http://www.kenyons.org

# APPENDIX ONE: UNDERSTANDING THE GIFTS

### 1. What is meant by Charismatic Gifts?

A charismatic gift is a manifestation of God's power and presence given freely, for God's honor and glory and for the service of others.

Specifically the term refers to manifestations of the power of the Holy Spirit mentioned in the Scriptures, especially after Pentecost, and which have always remained with the Church in both her teaching and practice.

### 2. How many Charismatic Gifts are there?

Since the charismatic gifts are manifestations of the Holy Spirit, it is impossible to say how many there are. Scripture provides a number of lists of offices and ministries. The classical list, used by most, is St. Paul's in 1 Corinthians 12:8-10, where nine gifts are described. These nine seem to be normal ministries that should be present in every local church.

### 3. A list and description of the Nine Gifts:

The nine gifts, according to the usual threefold division are:

## A. THE WORD GIFTS

*(The Power to Say)*

a) **The Gift of Tongues** – whereby the person gives God's message, in a language unknown to him, for the community present. This also includes a prayer language used for personal prayer. It is a multiple gift of languages.

b) **The Gift of Interpretation** – whereby a person, after the use of the gift of tongues, gives the general meaning of what the person has said, or a response to what has been said. Interpretation can also be used privately in conjunction with the gift of prayer tongues.

c) **The Gift of Prophecy** – whereby the person gives God's message in the vernacular for the community or for an individual.

## B. THE SIGN GIFTS

*(The Power To Do)*

a) **The Gift of faith** – which enables the person at a given moment to believe, and to call upon Gods' power with a certainty that excludes all doubt.

b) **The Gift of Healing** – which enables the person to be God's instrument in bringing about the well-being of another, on one or more levels, spiritual, psychological or physical.

c) **The Gift of Miracles** – which enables a person to be God's instrument in either an instant healing or in some other powerful manifestation of God's power.

## C. THE INTELLECTUAL GIFTS
### *(The Power to Know)*

a) **The Word of Wisdom** – whereby a person is granted an insight into God's plan in a given situation and is enabled to put into words of advice or of direction.

b) **The Word of Knowledge** – whereby a person is granted an insight into a divine mystery or facet of man's relation to God and is enabled to put this into a word that helps others to grasp the mystery.

c) **The Gift of Discernment** – whereby a person is enabled to know the source of an inspiration or action, whether it came from the Holy Spirit or from the evil spirit.

# APPENDIX TWO:
# PRAYER FOR
# THE BAPTISM IN THE SPIRIT

**Notes:** In preparing this book, one of the reviewers suggested that it would be of an advantage to have a prayer that one could use to ask for the Baptism in the Spirit. They asked: "What if people haven't received Holy Spirit?" "Where do they go for that prayer?"

Seeing that we think of this book as a course, we have added a prayer that you can use to ask for the in-filling of the Holy Spirit. This is the Gift from God the Father that Jesus referred to in Luke 24.

> **[48] You are witnesses of these things. [49] I am going to send you what my Father has promised; but stay in the city until you have been clothed with power from on high."**
> Luke 24:48-49

This is the last commandment given by Jesus before He ascended up into Heaven: that we are to be clothed with the power from on high – His Holy Spirit.

# THE PRAYER:

### 1. BECOME READY:

Take a moment to calm yourself, closing your eyes, clear your mind and become quiet before the Lord.

### 2. REPENT:

We need to become clean before the Lord. Ask the Lord if there is anything that needs repenting.

### 3. ACCEPT JESUS AS LORD: *(Pray this prayer.)*

*LORD JESUS, I ACCEPT YOU AS MY PERSONAL LORD AND SAVIOR. I PLACE YOU ON THE THRONE OF MY LIFE. I SURRENDER MY LIFE TO YOU. FROM NOW ON I BELONG TO YOU. I WANT TO WALK IN YOUR WAYS AND UNDER YOUR LORDSHIP ALL THE DAYS OF MY LIFE.*

### 4. YIELDING TO THE BAPTISM IN THE SPIRIT

*LORD, JESUS, NOW I AM READY. I HAVE EMPTIED MYSELF, REPENTED OF MY SINS AND PROCLAIMED YOU AS MY PERSONAL LORD AND SAVIOR. I ASK YOU TO FILL ME WITH THE LIVING WATERS OF YOUR SPIRIT. I CLAIM THE PROMISE YOU MADE, IF WE ASK WE WILL RECEIVE. I AM NOW ASKING LORD IN FAITH, COME HOLY SPIRIT AND BAPTIZE ME.*

## 5. THANK YOU PRAYER: *(Pray this prayer.)*

*FATHER, I THANK YOU FOR THE BAPTISM IN THE HOLY SPIRIT. I THANK YOU FATHER, FOR THIS TEACHING AS AN INTRODUCTION AND EXPLANATION OF WHO HOLY SPIRIT IS, WHAT HOLY SPIRIT DOES, AND HOW HE OPERATES IN ME AND THROUGH ME.*

*THANK YOU FOR A GREATER UNDERSTANDING OF THE NINE GIFTS DESCRIBED IN 1 CORINTHIANS 12 AND HOW THEY FUNCTION INDIVIDUALLY AND TOGETHER TO EQUIP ME FOR SERVICE TO YOU AND THE KINGDOM OF GOD IN POWER.*

*THANK YOU FOR OPENING THE EYES OF MY UNDERSTANDING AND THE DOOR OF MY HEART TO RECEIVE ALL THAT YOU HAVE FOR ME.*

*I PRAYER THAT, IN LOVE, I MIGHT SPEAK AND DO THOSE ACTS THAT BRING GLORY TO YOUR NAME.*

*IN THE NAME OF THE LORD JESUS. AMEN.*

# APPENDIX THREE:

# BRIEF BIOGRAPHY OF THOMAS WILLIAM ROYCROFT

This biography was graciously written by Barbara Roycroft the wife of Bill (William) Roycroft who followed in his father's footsteps as the pastor for the local Lethbridge church, Lethbridge Christian Tabernacle.

Thomas William Roycroft (1908-1981) was a large-hearted lover of Jesus and 'a prince among his brothers' in the City of Lethbridge, Alberta, Canada. He had a powerful healing and teaching ministry and his prayers moved mountains out of the lives of people to whom he ministered.

His book *You Can Minister Spiritual Gifts* became a valuable teaching resource for the body of Christ. He walked in the love and gracious grace of the Spirit, bring restoration and revelation by the Spirit to the broken lost and torn hearts that he found himself surrounded by.

In his apostolic and prophetic ministry he started many bible study and prayer groups, all around Southern Alberta communities. Our church, the Lethbridge Christian Tabernacle, was formed from a bible study group following a Leighton Ford Crusade (from the Billy Graham Association) in the late 50's early 60's. The Church was incorporated in 1967 and we are now over 50 years old and continue to flourish under the grace of the wonderful Holy Spirit.

Tom and Anne Roycroft had two sons, Fred (of Vancouver, B.C.) and Bill (William), many grandchildren and great grandchildren following behind.

Sincerely, Barb Roycroft *(daughter in-law)*

www.ingramcontent.com/pod-product-compliance
Lightning Source LLC
Chambersburg PA
CBHW050436010526
44118CB00013B/1546